Christine McFadden is a freelance cookery writer and editor, writing cookery books as well as articles about food and nutrition for various consumer magazines. Before this, she was a successful graphic designer. Her strong visual sense is carried through to her colourful recipes, as is her love of lively ingredients.

Christine is an enthusiastic herb and vegetable gardener and enjoys growing unusual plants. She lives in Bath with her husband, son and large cat, Woodstock.

Also by Christine McFadden

HEALTHY MAIN MEAL SALADS
NEW VEGETARIAN FOOD
COMBINED RECIPES FOR VEGETARIANS AND
   NON-VEGETARIANS
FRUGAL FEASTS

HEALTHY FRUIT DESSERTS

CHRISTINE McFADDEN

Photographs by Don Last

Little, Brown and Company
BOSTON NEW YORK TORONTO LONDON

A LITTLE, BROWN BOOK

First published in the United Kingdom
by Little, Brown and Company (UK) in 1996

A CIP catalogue for this book is available
from the British Library

ISBN 0 316 87830 8

Typeset by Solidus (Bristol) Limited
Printed and bound in Great Britain by
Clays Ltd, St Ives plc

Little, Brown and Company (UK)
Brettenham House
Lancaster Place
London WC2E 7EN

Contents

Acknowledgements

I would like to thank my husband, Ed, for putting up with a sticky kitchen and for uncomplainingly sampling winter puddings during a heatwave. Many thanks also to Jill Newsome and family, Anna Parry-Jones, Alex Roberts and Veronica Sperling for their invaluable feedback during the recipe testing, and to Emily Azis for kindly supplying quinces and medlars.

Introduction

From a health point of view, desserts are not strictly essential because we get all the nutrients we need from the rest of the meal, providing it contains plenty of vegetables. But most of us would probably admit that even a quick midweek supper does not feel like a proper meal unless it ends with a dessert, however simple. Desserts help satisfy a deep-seated desire for something sweet, and they make us feel good.

Desserts are tempting because more often than not they contain fat and sugar. Fat improves texture and flavour, and because it is digested slowly it makes us feel satisfied. Sweetness is one of the first tastes we experience as infants and we are instinctively drawn to it, especially if life isn't going too well. The dangers of excess fat in the diet are well known – it increases the risk of heart disease, obesity and some cancers. Sugar is not such a killer, but excess intake may lead to obesity and tooth decay.

Desserts made with fruit, however, are a different story. Fruit is packed with vitamins, minerals and fibre, so it's the perfect ingredient for health-promoting desserts which are every bit as tempting as those based on excessive amounts of fat and sugar. Fruit is also aptly named – the word comes from the Latin *frui*, meaning 'to enjoy or delight in'.

The fruits we most enjoy share one characteristic which sets them apart from other foods – they are all inherently sweet, or a pleasing combination of sweetness and acidity. Despite its sweetness, fruit is low in calories. For the simplest and healthiest dessert, eat fruit plain or as part of a luscious fruit salad. Combined with other ingredients, fruit can still be a mouthwatering but healthy treat.

When I embarked on this book, I began with low-fat versions of old favourites such as cheesecakes and mousses. Although some perfectly acceptable results emerged, I came to the conclusion that if a fruit dessert really needs a dollop of double cream, then double cream it must be; low-fat versions just will not do. And I think this is fine if you reserve cream for an occasional treat.

As the book progressed, however, it gradually dawned on me that fruit could be given the same treatment as vegetables. After all, we eat vegetables in the healthiest possible way – raw or lightly steamed, grilled or stir-fried; and we don't always make a point of smothering them with cream or encasing them in pastry. Fruit salads are a well-known dessert, but why not a fruit stir-fry or a frittata, or a fruit pizza or salsa? And why not experiment with a more adventurous choice of herbs and spices? After all, cinnamon is not the only spice which goes with fruit. At last I was making some headway.

Healthy Fruit Desserts will appeal therefore to a wide range of tastes. The recipes include healthy variations of traditional desserts enjoyed by old and young alike, as well as some unusual ideas for more adventurous palates. There are recipes for exquisite featherlight desserts for special occasions, as well as simpler dishes for family meals.

The recipes include desserts made with voguish exotic fruits, but there is greater emphasis on traditional seasonal fruits. In particular there are recipes which give neglected varieties such as quinces and medlars the recognition they deserve.

Some of the recipes draw on Elizabethan and Victorian themes where sweetly fragrant herbs, spices, flower essences and edible leaves and flowers are combined with fruit to complement its sweet-sharp flavour. Others draw on Middle Eastern cuisines in which nuts and whole grains are added to fruit for extra texture and substance. You'll even find some recipes with chillies – a surprisingly good combination with strongly flavoured fruit.

THE ULTIMATE SUPERFOOD

Together with vegetables, fruit is an essential component in a healthy diet. It contains a little protein, minuscule amounts of fat and, being mostly composed of water, very few calories. Fruits with dense flesh, such as bananas and plums, contain useful amounts of carbohydrate and are a good energy boost.

Fruit also provides essential bulk and fibre for the digestive system. Many fruits contain pectin, a type of fibre which has the beneficial effect of lowering blood cholesterol. Pectin-rich fruits include apples, quinces, medlars, blackcurrants and redcurrants, blackberries, raspberries, apricots and plums.

Fruit is a rich source of essential minerals and vitamins. All fruit is high in potassium, which we need for the balance of fluid within the cells and for healthy muscle function. It is correspondingly low in sodium – a good nutritional balance. Fruit also contains calcium, needed for healthy bones and teeth; magnesium, needed for muscle and nerve control; and iron, which produces a substance called haemoglobin to carry oxygen around the blood.

By far the most important nutrient in fruit is vitamin C, which we need for general good health and resistance to infection, and to help the body absorb iron from food. Fruit and vegetables are the only foods which supply vitamin C. Together with carotene (vitamin A) and vitamin E, vitamin C is a natural anti-oxidant which protects the body from free-radical damage. Free radicals are harmful molecules made up of unpaired electrons. In an attempt to find a partner, they break up existing pairs of electrons, damaging the cells as they do so.

Research has now established that the anti-oxidants play an essential role in the prevention of heart disease and some cancers.

The amount of vitamin C present in fruit varies according to the type, as well as length of storage and amount of exposure to light, air and heat. Blackcurrants are exceptionally rich in it, although some will be lost during cooking. Guavas, papayas, citrus fruits and strawberries are also excellent sources. Dried fruit doesn't contain any vitamin C, but it is a concentrated source of energy and fibre.

Most fruit contains the powerful anti-oxidant carotene, which the body converts to vitamin A. We need it for healthy skin and membranes and to fight infections. Orange-fleshed fruit such as mangoes, papayas and Canteloupe and Charentais melons are overflowing with it. Dried apricots are a particularly rich source.

Some fruits contain a small amount of vitamin B complex, a group of vitamins needed for the release of energy from food. Oranges, clementines, bananas, kiwi fruit, strawberries and raspberries are examples.

Bananas, melons, plums, gooseberries, figs, blackberries and mangoes contain a small amount of vitamin E, mainly found in vegetable oils, nuts, seeds, grains and egg yolk. Vitamin E is another anti-oxidant which helps increase resistance to viruses, harmful bacteria and some cancers.

MAKING DESSERTS HEALTHY

The recipes in this book endeavour to create the deep pleasure and satisfaction associated with desserts, without compromising healthy eating goals or the dessert's appeal. A piece of top-quality raw fruit or a simple fruit salad makes the healthiest dessert, but where fruit is combined with other ingredients the emphasis is on lightness and nutritional balance, without any compromise of enjoyment.

This means that sources of fat, such as butter, cream and egg yolk, are used only where essential to flavour and texture, and the amount per serving is kept small. I've used ricotta cheese, quark, smetana and buttermilk (see Glossary of Ingredients, page 219), all naturally low in fat and infinitely preferable to low-fat versions of high-fat products.

Fruit provides natural sweetness in the form of fructose, so I've used sugar and honey only when essential. I don't have a sweet tooth so the quantity added is small – you may feel you want to add more.

Grains such as polenta, rice and bulgar wheat go well with sharp-tasting fruit, and seeds and nuts make crunchy toppings and garnishes. These ingredients add protein, B vitamins, vitamin E, minerals and fibre.

Although I've sometimes used wholemeal flour in pastry to increase the fibre content, it is always combined with plain or self-raising white flour to give lightness. I've used vegetable oil instead of melted butter for brushing filo pastry – that way you'll be getting more vitamin E and less cholesterol. Choux pastry and yeasted doughs appear now and again: they're light-textured and low in fat.

Cooking methods which trap air are a great way of cutting down on fat and making a little go a long way. Whisked sponges make almost fat-free flan bases, and whisking extra egg whites and reducing the number of yolks in egg-based dishes makes a wonderfully light but satisfying and tempting result.

CHOOSING FRUIT

The secret to choosing perfect fruit is to learn to recognize when it is at the peak of its growth cycle. Fruit picked too early will never develop fully those luscious flavours and textures which so delight the taste-buds. Thanks to modern packaging, storage and transportation methods, most fruit is available all year round, but strawberries in June somehow taste better than strawberries at Christmas. So it's also useful to know when different varieties are in their proper season. The sections on individual fruits at the beginning of each chapter will give you some guidance on seasons and how to recognize a fruit at the peak of ripeness.

STORING FRUIT

From the moment of harvest, fruit begins to lose its flavour and nutritional value. Fully ripe fruit should be eaten within a day or two of purchase. Otherwise, store it in the salad drawer of the fridge (except bananas which will turn black), or in a cool airy larder. Most unripe fruit can be kept at room temperature and will continue to ripen.

PREPARING FRUIT

For maximum nutritional benefit, fruit is best eaten raw, as vitamins are partially destroyed by heat. But tart fruits like blackcurrants, rhubarb and quinces need cooking to make them palatable. To avoid loss of nutrients:

* Wash fruit quickly – soaking causes vitamins to leach into the water.
* Avoid peeling unless absolutely necessary. The skin provides fibre as well as vitamins, which are often concentrated just below the surface.
* Prepare fruit just before you cook it, or, if raw, just before you eat it. Exposing cut surfaces to the air causes nutrients to oxidize, and in some cases discoloration.
* Use minimum water for stewing and cook for the shortest time possible. Keep the juice to serve with the fruit.

COOKERY NOTES

All eggs are size 3 unless otherwise specified.
All spoon measures are level.

CONVERSION TABLES

Quantities in the recipes are given in metric and imperial. Oven temperatures are in centigrade (for both conventional and fan ovens) and gas. The following tables show approximate equivalents between metric, imperial and American measures, together with Fahrenheit oven temperature equivalents.

Approximate Weight and Volume Equivalents

Commodity	Metric	Imperial	American
Almonds: whole	40 g	1½ oz	⅓ cup
ground	25 g	1 oz	⅓ cup
Apples, peeled and sliced	100 g	4 oz	1 cup
Apricots, dried	175 g	6 oz	1 cup
Bananas, sliced	175 g	6 oz	1 cup
Butter	225 g	8 oz	2 sticks
	25 g	1 oz	2 tbsp
Cheese: cottage	225 g	8 oz	1 cup
ricotta	225 g	8 oz	1 cup
Cocoa powder	25 g	1 oz	¼ cup
Cranberries	100 g	4 oz	1 cup
Cream	225 ml	8 fl oz	1 cup
Currants, dried	150 g	5 oz	1 cup
Flour (sifted)	150 g	5 oz	1 cup
Milk	225 ml	8 fl oz	1 cup
Oats, rolled	75 g	3 oz	1 cup
Pine kernels	25 g	1 oz	¼ cup
Pistachio nuts, shelled	50 g	2 oz	⅓ cup

Commodity	Metric	Imperial	American
Polenta	150 g	5 oz	1 cup
Prunes	200 g	7 oz	1 cup
Rhubarb, trimmed and sliced	450 g	1 lb	2½ cups
Rice, short-grain, uncooked	100 g	4 oz	½cup
Strawberries, whole	150 g	5 oz	1 cup
Suet, shredded	50 g	2 oz	½ cup
Sugar: granulated, caster, demerara	100 g	4 oz	½ cup
icing (confectioner's)	50 g	2 oz	½ cup
Tapioca	75 g	3 oz	½ cup
Walnut halves	40 g	1½ oz	½ cup

Fahrenheit Oven Temperature Equivalents

Centigrade °	Fahrenheit °	Gas
110	225	¼
120	250	½
140	275	1
150	300	2
170	325	3
180	350	4
190	375	5
200	400	6
220	425	7
230	450	8
240	475	9

Desserts with Orchard Fruit

This chapter features desserts made with traditional orchard fruit – apples, pears, quinces and medlars. Many of the recipes are healthier versions of old favourites, but you'll find some new ideas too, using sweet spices, herbs and fragrant syrups.

APPLES

Without question, apples must be one of the most popular fruits. There are now over 3000 named varieties, of which probably only fifty are available, so it's encouraging to see the major supermarkets stocking a wider range of old-fashioned apples. That said, you'll probably find specialist fruit farms a better bet for the more unusual varieties.

I have never understood the British tendency to classify apples as cookers and eaters. Most eating apples cook well and keep their texture, producing a stiffer purée. Unless you specifically want the soft purée produced by cookers, try experimenting with crisp, full-flavoured eating apples – English Cox's, Egremont Russets and Braeburns from New Zealand are all good.

Choose apples with a smooth, unblemished skin. Those

with red skins tend to have a woolly flesh, while mottled or green-skinned apples are crisper. A ripe apple will usually have an appley aroma but sometimes there is no knowing. My advice is to buy them from a reliable greengrocer or a supermarket known for its top-quality produce. Keep apples in the fridge, only transferring them to the fruit bowl on the day you want to eat them. Firm-fleshed varieties can be kept for several weeks if individually wrapped and stored on racks in a cool airy place.

While not a major source of any particular nutrient, apples are refreshing to eat and are a reasonable source of fibre, vitamins C and E, and some minerals.

Source	Season
Chile	March–July
France	October–March
Holland	September–April
New Zealand	April–August
South Africa	March–September
United Kingdom	August–May
United States	September–April

PEARS

Pears must come a close second to apples in popularity but they are more temperamental to deal with. They ripen very quickly from the core outwards and are at their peak for a short period of time. Pears need handling with care as they bruise very easily. A ripe pear has a distinctive aroma, and is slightly soft around the base of the stalk. Pears can be kept in the fridge or a cool cellar for a few days.

As with apples, there are thousands of varieties, ranging from the greenish-russet Conference with its juicy but gritty flesh, to the superb yellow-skinned Comice, meltingly soft and dripping with juice. Firm-fleshed varieties are better for cooking and make beautiful autumn puddings.

Pears are a reasonable source of energy-giving carbohydrate, fibre, vitamins C and E, and minerals.

Source	Season
Australia	March–June
Chile	March–June
France	July–April
Holland	August–April
South Africa	February–July
United Kingdom	September–June

QUINCES

Quinces are one of my favourite fruits. There is something magical about the way they hang in the tree like golden orbs long after the leaves have fallen, and the way a bowl of quinces can perfume a room with the most exquisite fragrance. They are quite hard to find unless you have access to a Greek greengrocer or are lucky enough to own a quince tree. Fortunately there seems to be some rekindling of interest among gardeners and food writers, which is to be encouraged. I suspect the problem is the difficulty of preparation. Quinces are tough skinned, hard fleshed and need long slow cooking to make them palatable – but are well worth the effort. A few slices added to an apple or pear dish will bring out the flavour of the fruit.

Store quinces in the same way as apples, making sure any with bruises or blemishes are kept well away from their neighbours.

Quinces are extremely rich in pectin, which is a form of dietary fibre, and are a useful source of potassium and calcium. They contain a reasonable amount of vitamin C too, but the lengthy cooking time means that much of this will be destroyed by heat.

Source	Season
Spain	October–November
United Kingdom	October–November

MEDLARS

Even more curious than the quince, the medlar is probably our oldest orchard fruit, dating back to Greek times and rarely seen nowadays. The greenish-brown fruits resemble giant rosehips and were rudely nicknamed by Chaucer 'openarse', because of their large open calyx.

Medlars become palatable only after a period of post-harvest decay known as 'bletting', during which the flesh turns a soft golden brown. Store them in a cool airy place for two or three weeks, keeping them separate from each other.

I have a feeling that this ancient fruit is coming back into favour, so I have included one or two recipes in the hope that readers with medlar trees will continue to use them.

The medlar's nutritional properties were appreciated in the early 1900s when doctors recommended the fruit as a valuable cure for digestive problems. It contains high levels of fibre, carbohydrate and potassium.

Source	Season
United Kingdom	October–November

SPICED BAKED APPLES

SERVES 4

I have never been a great fan of baked apples – tough skins and mushy insides put me off. But made with peeled crisp eating apples, this is an entirely different experience.

4 tbsp raisins
2 tbsp sunflower seeds
40 g/1½ oz almonds with skin, roughly chopped
finely grated zest of ½ orange
crushed seeds from 6 cardamom pods
¼ tsp freshly grated nutmeg
pinch ground cloves
6 tbsp clear honey
4 large Braeburn or Cox's apples
small knob of butter
150 ml/¼ pint apple juice

Mix together the raisins, sunflower seeds, almonds, orange zest, cardamom and other spices. Stir in the honey, mixing well.

Using an apple corer, neatly core the apples all the way through, then peel them and smear with butter.

Place the apples in a roasting tin into which they will fit snugly. Spoon over the honey mixture, allowing some of the dried fruit and nuts to spill into the core holes.

Bake in a preheated oven at 200°C (190°C fan oven)/gas 6 for 50–60 minutes, basting frequently, until tender.

Using a slotted spoon, remove the apples, dried fruit and nuts to a serving dish and keep warm. Pour the apple juice into the roasting tin. Place over a medium heat and bring to the boil, scraping up all the crusty bits from the bottom of the pan, just as you would for gravy. Simmer until reduced slightly. Pour over the apples and serve at once.

APPLES IN LEMON BALM JELLY

SERVES 4

This makes a refreshing dessert after a heavy meal. If possible use Braeburn apples, which turn a luminous pale gold as they hang suspended in the translucent jelly. You could use mint instead of lemon balm.

225 g / 8 oz sugar
850 ml / 1½ pints water
finely grated zest of 1 lemon
2 large crisp eating apples
1 sachet powdered gelatine
1 tbsp finely chopped fresh lemon balm
fresh lemon balm leaves, to decorate
satsuma segments, to decorate

Put the sugar, water and lemon zest in a saucepan and dissolve the sugar over a low heat.

Peel the apples and cut in half horizontally. Slice a thin piece from the top and bottom so that they stand flat with the widest part uppermost. Dig out the core.

Add the apples to the sugar syrup. Simmer for 10 minutes, covered, turning over halfway through. Remove from the heat and leave to cool in the syrup.

Put 4 tablespoons of boiling water in a small bowl. Sprinkle the gelatine over the surface and leave to stand for 10 minutes until spongy. Place over a pan of hot water until fully dissolved.

Drain the apples, reserving the syrup, and place in individual glass serving bowls.

Measure the syrup, adding water if necessary to make up to 600 ml / 1 pint.

Add the dissolved gelatine to the syrup, mixing thoroughly.

Stir in the lemon balm and pour over the apples. Leave in the fridge to set.

Decorate with a lemon balm leaf and one or two skinned satsuma segments.

TWO-APPLE PIZZA WITH ORANGE AND CINNAMON

SERVES 8

There is no reason why a pizza cannot be sweet; the principles are the same as for a savoury one – very high heat and a light topping, so that the base is cooked through and crisp. For the best results, use a perforated pizza pan, or better still, a preheated pizza stone. Here I've combined cooking and eating apples – a fluffy purée of cooking apples is topped with caramelized segments of crisp eating apples. Unlike ordinary pastry, yeasted dough contains hardly any fat.

400 g / 14 oz cooking apples, peeled, cored and roughly chopped
finely grated zest of ½ lemon
finely grated zest of ½ orange
sugar, to taste
¼ tsp ground cinnamon
knob of butter
350 g / 12 oz crisp eating apples, such as Braeburn or Cox's
lemon juice
1 quantity Rich Yeast Dough (page 197)
almond or grapeseed oil, for brushing
40 g / 1½ oz dried cherries
25 g / 1 oz flaked almonds

Put the prepared cooking apples in a small saucepan with the lemon and orange zest, and 3 tablespoons of water. Cover and simmer over a low heat for 7–10 minutes, stirring occasionally to prevent burning, until reduced to a thick purée. Stir in sugar to taste, the cinnamon and the butter.

Quarter, core and peel the eating apples, then slice each piece lengthways into very thin segments, sprinkling with lemon juice as you prepare them.

Roll out the dough to a 30 cm/12 inch circle and place on a perforated pizza pan. Pinch up the edges to make a raised rim, then lightly brush all over with oil. Spread the apple purée thinly over the base. Arrange the segments on top in concentric circles. Brush lightly with oil, then sprinkle with sugar.

Bake in a preheated oven at 240°C (230°C fan oven)/gas 9 for 15 minutes until the apples begin to blacken at the edges. Scatter the cherries and almonds over the top, and bake for 2 minutes more. Sprinkle with a little more sugar and serve at once.

APPLE, LEMON AND MINT FRITTATA

SERVES 6

A fruity version of what is normally a thick savoury omelette. Cold wedges of leftovers make a deeply satisfying snack for late-night fridge-raiders. This recipe contains half the usual amount of egg yolks, which considerably reduces the cholesterol content.

4 eggs (size 2)
4 egg whites (size 2)
1½–2 tbsp sugar
finely grated zest of 1 lemon
1 tbsp chopped fresh mint
350 g / 12 oz crisp eating apples, such as Braeburn or Cox's
juice of ½ lemon
1 tbsp grapeseed oil
25 g / 1 oz butter

Beat the whole eggs and the whites with 1 tablespoon of the sugar, the lemon zest and mint.

Quarter, core and peel the apples, then cut the quarters crossways into segments. Put in a bowl with the lemon juice to prevent discoloration.

Heat the oil and butter in a 24–25 cm / 9½–10 inch non-stick frying pan. Add the apples, sprinkle with some of the remaining sugar and fry over a high heat for 6–8 minutes, shaking the pan continuously and carefully turning the slices with tongs until they are golden.

Lower the heat and add the egg mixture, stirring to distribute the apples evenly. Cook over a medium heat for 7–8 minutes until almost set.

Slide the frittata on to a plate, cover with the pan, then invert it back into the pan. Briefly return to the heat to brown the second side.

Sprinkle with the remaining sugar, cut into wedges and serve warm or at room temperature.

APPLE, PRUNE AND WALNUT FILO TART

SERVES 8–10

Delicious served hot or at room temperature, this makes a lovely finish to an autumnal dinner. Start the day before you plan to serve it, to allow time for soaking the prunes. For a real zing, soak them in Armagnac instead of tea, or, as a compromise, mix with 4 tablespoons of Armagnac after chopping. Crisp, golden and healthily low in fat, filo pastry is a delicious alternative to ordinary pastry. Here it is lightly dabbed with oil instead of the more usual coating of melted butter.

275 g/10 oz prunes
450 ml/¾ pint cold Earl Grey tea
100 g/4 oz walnuts
1 kg/2¼ lb crisp eating apples, quartered, cored, peeled and thickly sliced
75 g/3 oz sugar
1 vanilla pod, split lengthways
finely grated zest of 1 lemon
finely grated zest of ½ orange
almond or grapeseed oil, for brushing
8 sheets filo pastry, measuring 35.5 ×30 cm/14 × 12 inches
1 tbsp orange-flower water
2 tbsp icing sugar

Put the prunes in a bowl and cover with cold tea. Leave to soak overnight.

Put the nuts on to a baking sheet and toast in a preheated moderate oven for about 5 minutes until golden and fragrant. Rub in a clean tea-towel to get rid of the skins, then chop finely and set aside.

Put the prepared apples in a heavy-based saucepan with the sugar, vanilla pod and lemon and orange zest. Cover and simmer over a very low heat for 20–25 minutes until soft.

Drain the prunes, reserving the soaking liquid. Chop the flesh roughly and mix with 4 tablespoons of the soaking liquid, or Armagnac.

Brush or spray with oil a 5 cm/2 inch deep baking dish measuring 25 × 20 cm/10 × 8 inches. Lay a sheet of filo in the base, allowing it to drape over the sides. Lightly brush with oil and sprinkle with a few chopped walnuts. Add another 3 sheets of filo, dabbing with oil and sprinkling walnuts between the layers.

Spread the prunes over the filo and top with the apples. Cover with the remaining filo, oiling each layer and sprinkling with walnuts. Trim the top layers to fit the dish. Sprinkle the top layer with the orange-flower water and icing sugar.

Bake in a preheated oven at 200°C (190°C fan oven)/gas 6 for 40–50 minutes until golden.

APPLE AND RAISIN SUET CRISP

SERVES 4–6

I found this recipe written on a scrap of paper in the post office and couldn't resist trying it. The unknown author specified golden syrup for the topping, but I have used date syrup (available from healthfood shops) as it is less cloyingly sweet, but it's up to you. I've also added some spices and citrus zest to sharpen up the flavour. You could add a few pieces of quince for a magic touch. Serve with Vanilla Custard (page 209). Suet pastry is not the most health-promoting of doughs, but it does make a deliciously comforting winter pud. Using vegetable suet reduces the saturated fat content, and wholemeal flour adds extra fibre.

100 g / 4 oz self-raising flour
100 g / 4 oz wholemeal self-raising flour
½ tsp salt
100 g / 4 oz shredded vegetable suet
finely grated zest of 1½ lemons
600 g / 1¼ lb crisp eating apples
1 tbsp lemon juice
40 g / 1½ oz raisins
finely grated zest of ½ orange
¼ tsp ground cinnamon
¼ tsp freshly grated nutmeg
pinch of ground cloves
4–5 tbsp date syrup
50 g / 2 oz unrefined demerara sugar

Sift the flours and salt into a bowl, adding the bran from the wholemeal flour. Add the suet and the zest of 1 lemon. Stirring with a fork, gradually mix in about 150 ml/¼ pint water. Knead briefly to form a firm dough.

Lightly grease a 18 × 25 cm/7 × 10 inch baking dish or roasting tin. Divide the dough in half. Roll each piece on a lightly floured work surface to a thin rectangle to fit the dish. Trim the edges neatly, and place a layer of pastry in the bottom of the dish.

Quarter, core, peel and slice the apples. Put in a bowl with the lemon juice, raisins, orange zest and remaining lemon zest, and the spices. Toss to mix.

Scatter the apple mixture over the pastry to form a thick layer. Cover with the second piece of pastry, lightly pressing it with the palm of your hand to flatten.

Pour the syrup over the pastry to cover the entire surface, then sprinkle with most of the sugar. Bake in a preheated oven at 190°C (180°C fan oven)/gas 5 for 40–45 minutes until dark brown and crisp. Sprinkle with a little more sugar and serve warm.

GREEN FRUIT SALAD WITH GINGER SYRUP

SERVES 6

A very pretty and refreshing salad with a subtle hint of ginger.
It looks lovely with a scattering of fresh raspberries and perhaps
a few tiny sprigs of ginger mint.

4 green-skinned crisp apples, unpeeled
lemon juice
1 Galia or Ogen melon
3 kiwi fruit, thinly sliced
175 g/6 oz seedless green grapes
1 quantity light Sugar Syrup (page 210) made with 3 finely chopped
slices of fresh ginger root

Quarter the apples and remove the cores. Slice lengthways into
thin segments. Put in a serving bowl and sprinkle with a little
lemon juice to prevent discoloration.

Cut the melon flesh into balls with a melon-baller (pages
132–3). Add to the bowl along with the kiwi fruit and grapes.

Pour over the cold syrup, straining it first if you do not
appreciate bursts of fresh ginger.

FAMILY FRUIT SALAD

SERVES 6

So-called because the fruits in this quickly made apple-based salad are the only ones my son likes. There are loud complaints if I try to sneak in other kinds. We make a huge bowl of it every few days to eat as a snack, as a healthy fruit dessert or to go with breakfast cereal. The strawberries are an optional extra – worth adding for their high vitamin C content. The salad will keep in the fridge for a few days, but in this case add the bananas just before serving, otherwise they will go brown.

4 crisp apples, such as Braeburn, Granny Smith or Cox's, unpeeled
2 bananas, sliced
juice of 1 lemon
juice of 4 oranges
150 g/5 oz each red and green seedless grapes
225 g/8 oz strawberries, sliced (optional)
3–4 tbsp elderflower syrup or pear juice concentrate

Quarter the apples and remove the cores. Slice crossways into thin segments. Put in a large serving bowl with the bananas and mix with the lemon juice to prevent discoloration.

Add the orange juice, grapes, and the strawberries if using. Stir in the elderflower syrup or the pear juice concentrate – they add a lovely flavour to the juice.

POACHED PEARS IN LAVENDER SYRUP

SERVES 4

When I was dreaming up this recipe I had a mental picture of translucent white pears floating in a lavender-blue syrup. I was mildly disappointed when the syrup turned out to be pale golden. However, the flavour is indescribably delicious – not exactly how lavender smells, but something closer to how I imagine nectar to taste. Serve at room temperature, perhaps with a scoop of best-quality vanilla ice-cream.

6 Conference pears
juice of ½ lemon
about 300 ml / ½ pint Lavender Syrup (page 216)

Quarter, core and peel the pears, tossing them with the lemon juice in a bowl. Then put them in a saucepan.

Heat the lavender syrup and pour it over the pears. There should be enough syrup to barely cover them. Bring to the boil, then cover and simmer gently for about 10 minutes, until the pears are translucent and tender.

Using a slotted spoon, remove the pears to a serving dish, taking care not to break them up. Boil the juices down for a few minutes until syrupy, then pour over the pears. Allow to cool before serving. Serve at room temperature.

VARIATION

Pears in Blackcurrant Syrup Use Blackcurrant Syrup (page 213) instead of Lavender Syrup, and add a split vanilla pod to the pears in the pan. Check the sweetness of the syrup when cool, and add a little more sugar if necessary. Scatter with slivers of whole almonds with skin.

GRILLED PEARS WITH ORANGE AND GREEN PEPPERCORN BUTTER

SERVES 4

Green peppercorns add a subtle smoky flavour to the juices. This has to be made with butter – low-fat spread just will not do – but there is a very small amount per serving.

4 Conference pears
juice of ½ lemon
50 g / 2 oz unsalted butter
finely grated zest of ½ orange
½ tsp dried green peppercorns, crushed
sugar, for sprinkling

Halve the pears lengthways, peel them and scoop out the cores. Put them in a bowl and toss with the lemon juice as you prepare them.

Mash the butter with the orange zest and green peppercorns.

Arrange the pear halves, flat side up, in a shallow ovenproof dish into which they will fit snugly in a single layer.

Put a small knob of butter in the cavity of each pear half, and sprinkle the edges with sugar.

Place the dish under a preheated very hot grill for 10–12 minutes until the pears are tender and beginning to blacken round the edges, and the juices are bubbling.

Serve hot with some of the buttery juices.

PEAR FANS WITH STRAWBERRY DRESSING

SERVES 4

This very simple dessert needs top-quality fruit with an intense flavour.

100 g / 4 oz strawberries, chopped
1 tsp sugar
juice of 1 lemon
4 dessert pears
strawberry slices, to decorate
coarsely ground black pepper
fresh mint sprigs, to decorate

Put the strawberries in a blender with the sugar and 1 teaspoon of the lemon juice. Purée for 2 minutes until smooth and thoroughly blended.

Halve the pears lengthways leaving the stalk intact. Peel them with a small sharp knife, and cut out the cores. With the cut side down and holding the knife at a 45-degree angle, cut each half lengthways into 6 slices, stopping short at the stalk end so they are still attached. Dip them in the remaining lemon juice.

Carefully place 2 pear halves on individual serving plates. Spread the slices out slightly to form a fan. Spoon over a little strawberry dressing and decorate with one or two strawberry slices. Add a light grinding of black pepper and top with a mint sprig. Serve at once.

SAUTÉED PEARS

SERVES 4

Use ripe pears with a good flavour and firm flesh – Conference would be a good choice. Shake the pan and toss the pears gently so that they don't break up. If you don't have lavender syrup, use clear honey instead, but don't boil it first. This is absolutely divine with some very cold ice-cream.

150 ml/¼ pint Lavender Syrup (page 216) or 3 tbsp clear honey
4 firm-fleshed pears
juice of ½ lemon
50 g/2 oz unsalted butter

Put the lavender syrup, if using, in a small saucepan and boil hard for 5 minutes until very syrupy.

Quarter, core and peel the pears, then slice each quarter lengthways into thin segments.

Heat the butter in a large frying pan until foaming. Add the pears and fry for 5–7 minutes, gently tossing them to turn, until golden on all sides.

Spoon over the lavender syrup or honey, and stir until the bubbling dies down. Take care not to break up the segments. Pour into a heated serving dish, scraping up all the sticky sediment and adding it to the dish.

PEAR AND GINGER PANCAKES

SERVES 4

I rarely think of making pancakes until Shrove Tuesday, but they are so delicious and easy that they could be a year-round treat. Orchard fruit poached in a fragrant syrup makes an ideal filling. Serve with the syrupy juices and a blob of vanilla-flavoured Low-Fat Thick Cream (page 207) or Ricotta Cream (page 206).

1 quantity Pancake Batter (page 202)
2 tbsp lemon juice
50 g/2 oz sugar
1 vanilla pod, split lengthways
4 pears, peeled, cored and sliced
1.5 cm/½ inch piece stem ginger, very finely chopped

Make 8 pancakes following the pancake batter recipe and keep warm.

Put the lemon juice, sugar, vanilla pod and pears in a large saucepan. Add just enough water to cover the pears. Stir gently over a low heat until the sugar has dissolved. Bring to the boil, then simmer gently for about 7 minutes until the pears are translucent and tender.

Remove the pears with a slotted spoon and set aside. Bubble down the juices until syrupy.

Place a few pear slices down the centre of each pancake. Sprinkle with the stem ginger. Roll up and place in a heated serving dish. Pour over the syrup and serve at once.

PEAR AND CRANBERRY COMPOTE WITH WALNUTS

SERVES 4–6

Use a firm-fleshed dessert pear such as Anjou, Conference or Bosc. The white flesh contrasts beautifully with the brilliant red cranberries.

6 pears
juice of 1 lemon
225 ml/8 fl oz white grape juice
50 g/2 oz sugar, or to taste
1 vanilla pod, split lengthways
4 cardamom pods
75 g/3 oz cranberries
chopped toasted walnuts, to decorate

Peel and core the pears, using an apple corer inserted from the bottom, then cut them in half lengthways. Brush with a little lemon juice to prevent discoloration.

Put the grape juice, sugar, vanilla and cardamom pods in a saucepan. Stir over a medium heat until the sugar has dissolved. Add the pears and lemon juice, and bring to the boil. Cover and simmer for 12–15 minutes, turning the pears over halfway through.

Remove the pears with a slotted spoon and transfer to a serving dish. Fish out the vanilla and cardamom.

Add the cranberries to the pan and simmer briskly for 5 minutes. Pour the cranberries and the juice over the pears. Allow to cool. Sprinkle with toasted walnuts before serving.

QUINCE AND MINT SORBET

SERVES 8

Quince and mint with a dash of stem ginger are the most heavenly combination of flavours. Use a strongly flavoured mint, such as spearmint or peppermint, and add it during the final beating, before the sorbet is frozen solid.

600 g / 1¼ lb quinces
1 quantity medium Sugar Syrup (page 210)
3 tbsp gin
3 tbsp chopped fresh mint
finely chopped stem ginger, to decorate
fresh mint sprigs, to decorate

Peel the quinces and cut into segments. Cut out the cores and slice the flesh.

Put the slices in a saucepan with 700 ml / 1¼ pints of water. Bring to the boil, then simmer over a low heat for about 50 minutes until soft. You may need to add a bit more water.

Drain the quinces, put in a blender or food processor and purée until smooth.

Boil the syrup hard for 5 minutes. Allow to cool then stir in the quince purée and gin. Pour into a freezerproof container and freeze for several hours until the mixture begins to harden around the edges.

Transfer to a deep bowl and whisk until smooth. If you have time, freeze again until hard around the edges, then whisk again. Add the mint during the last whisking. Freeze overnight until solid.

Remove the sorbet from the freezer 30 minutes before serving. Serve in individual glass bowls and decorate each with a little stem ginger and a tiny sprig of mint.

QUINCES IN LIME JELLY

SERVES 4

A very pretty dessert of rosy-pink quinces floating in a translucent pale pink jelly.

2 large quinces
225 g / 8 oz sugar
850 ml / 1½ pints water
1 sachet powdered gelatine
finely grated zest of 2 limes
blackberries or blueberries, to decorate

Peel the quinces and cut in half horizontally through the widest point. Slice a piece from the top and bottom so that the quinces stand flat with the widest part uppermost.

Put the sugar and water in a saucepan and dissolve the sugar over a medium heat. Add the quinces to the syrup. Cover and simmer for 40 minutes, turning over halfway through. Add a little more water if necessary. Remove from the heat and leave the quinces to cool in the syrup.

Drain the quinces, reserving the syrup, and place in individual glass serving bowls.

Measure the syrup, adding water if necessary to make up to 600 ml / 1 pint.

Pour 4 tablespoons of boiling water into a small bowl. Sprinkle the gelatine over the surface and leave for 10 minutes until spongy. Place over a pan of hot water until fully dissolved. Add to the syrup, mixing well. Stir in the lime zest.

Pour the syrup over the quinces. Leave in the fridge to set. Decorate with a few blackberries or blueberries before serving.

QUINCE AND ANISE MOUSSE

SERVES 4

This low-fat but creamy mousse is made with yogurt and silken tofu. It contains uncooked egg white, so keep it chilled and eat within 24 hours. Serve with thin vanilla biscuits, such as Langues de Chat.

2 large quinces
200 g/7 oz sugar
finely grated zest and juice of 1 lemon
seeds from 1 star anise pod, crushed
100 ml/3½ fl oz Greek yogurt
100 g/4 oz silken tofu
1 tbsp powdered gelatine
2 egg whites (size 2)
blackberries, to decorate

Peel and core the quinces, then cut into segments. Put in a saucepan with 150 g/5 oz of the sugar and 1 L/1¾ pints of water. Bring to the boil, then simmer for at least 1 hour until soft. Drain the quinces and purée in a food processor or blender until smooth.

Transfer the mixture to a bowl, then stir in the lemon zest and juice, the anise and the remaining sugar.

Mix together the yogurt and tofu, then push through a sieve. Stir into the quince purée.

Put 8 tablespoons of boiling water in a small bowl. Scatter the gelatine over the surface and leave for 10 minutes until spongy. Place over a pan of hot water until completely dissolved, then add to the quince mixture, mixing well.

Whisk the egg whites until stiff. Stir about one-third into the quince mixture to slacken it, then lightly fold in the rest with a metal spoon. Divide the mixture among 4 serving bowls and chill for 2–3 hours until set.

Decorate with a few blackberries just before serving.

SPICED QUINCE AND CRANBERRY FILO TART

SERVES 8

An impressive winter dessert of deep pink quinces and ruby red cranberries, perfect for a dinner party or a delicious alternative to Christmas pudding. You'd think this was a wickedly indulgent pud, but the filo case and ricotta cream make it surprisingly low in fat. Smetana is another really good low-fat alternative to cream, made from skimmed milk, single cream and a souring agent. It's available from good supermarkets and deserves to be used more often.

500 g/1¼ lb quinces
150 g/5 oz sugar
1 vanilla pod
7.5 cm/3 inch cinnamon stick
5 cardamom pods, crushed
75 g/3 oz cranberries
6 sheets filo pastry measuring 24 cm/9½ inch square
grapeseed or almond oil, for brushing
25 g/1 oz chopped mixed nuts
2 tbsp icing sugar
1 tbsp orangeflower water or rosewater
300 ml/½ pint Ricotta Cream (page 206) or smetana

Peel the quinces, saving the peel. Cut lengthways into eighths. If the segments are very thick, cut in half lengthways again. Remove the cores and reserve with the peel.

Heat 1 L/1¾ pints of water with the sugar, vanilla, cinnamon and cardamom. When the sugar has dissolved, add the quinces. Bring to the boil, then cover and simmer over a low heat for 1½ hours until the quinces are soft and have turned a deep rosy pink.

Add the cranberries and simmer for another 5 minutes. Remove from the heat and allow to cool in the syrup.

Drain the fruit, pouring the juice back into the saucepan. Add the reserved peelings and cores to the juice. Boil for 20 minutes until reduced to a jelly-like syrup. Strain into a jug and leave to cool.

Cover the filo sheets with a clean damp tea towel. Taking one sheet at a time, dab with oil and place in a lightly greased 4 cm/1½ inch deep loose-bottomed flan tin, 23 cm/9 inch in diameter. Sprinkle with some of the nuts, then place the next sheet on top, rotating it so that the corners are offset. Gently press the pastry into the edge of the tin. The corners of the pastry should stick up above the rim like the petals of a flower.

Mix the icing sugar and orangeflower water to a paste and use to paint the pastry petals.

Bake the pastry case in a preheated oven at 190°C (180°C fan oven)/gas 5 for 10–15 minutes until golden and crisp. Allow to cool then carefully ease out of the tin.

Spread the ricotta cream over the base of the pastry case. Arrange the quince slices on top in concentric overlapping circles. Scatter with the cranberries, then spoon the cooled syrup over the top.

QUINCE AND GINGER TART

SERVES 4–6

A quickly prepared tart in which the quinces are cooked in the pastry shell without pre-poaching. They turn a beautiful shade of golden pink during baking. Slice the flesh as thinly as possible so that it cooks all the way through. Don't prick the base of the pastry case, otherwise the juices will leak.

1 quantity All-in-One Shortcrust Pastry (page 192)
lightly beaten egg white, for brushing
450 g / 1 lb quinces (350 g / 12 oz when peeled and cored)
1 tbsp cornflour
75 g / 3 oz sugar
1 knob of stem ginger, very finely chopped
2 tbsp ginger syrup from the jar
juice of 1 large orange
1 quantity light Sugar Syrup (page 210)

Roll out the pastry on a lightly floured surface to form a circle 3 mm/1/8 inch thick. Use to line a 20 cm/8 inch tart tin with a removable base. Chill for 30 minutes.

Line the pastry case with foil and baking beans. Bake in a preheated oven at 200°C (190°C fan oven)/gas 6 for 20 minutes. Remove the foil and beans and bake for 5 minutes more. Leave to cool, then paint with beaten egg white. This helps prevent the base becoming soggy when the filling is added.

Peel the quinces, reserving the peel, and slice each length-ways into 8 segments. Remove the cores, and reserve with the peel. Cut the flesh crossways into thin slices.

Put the quince slices in a bowl with the cornflour, sugar and stem ginger. Toss thoroughly so that the slices are well coated.

Leave to stand for about 10 minutes until the juices begin to flow a little.

Arrange the quince slices in the pastry case in overlapping circles. Spoon over the ginger syrup and orange juice.

Bake in the oven at 200°C (190°C fan oven)/gas 6 for about 1 hour, until the quinces are soft and just beginning to blacken at the edges.

Meanwhile put the reserved peel and cores in a small saucepan with the syrup. Simmer for 30 minutes until jelly-like. Strain and set aside.

Remove the tart from the oven and spoon the syrup over the quinces to glaze. Serve warm or at room temperature.

SPICED MEDLAR TART WITH WALNUT PASTRY

SERVES 6–8

The pleasantly astringent flavour of this autumnal tart will keep your friends guessing. Make sure the medlars are well bletted – the flesh should be dark orangey-brown and very soft.

1 quantity Nut Pastry made with walnuts (page 193)
750 g/1 lb 10 oz bletted medlars
75 g/3 oz caster sugar
½ tsp ground cinnamon
½ tsp ground ginger
¼ tsp freshly grated nutmeg
¼ tsp salt
3 eggs
150 ml/¼ pint single cream
sieved icing sugar, to decorate
Ricotta Cream (page 206), whipped cream or thick yogurt, to serve

Press the pastry into a 23 cm/9 inch tart tin with a removable base, working it well into the sides with the edge of your index finger. The base should be about 3 mm/⅛ inch thick and the sides 5 mm/¼ inch thick. Chill for 30 minutes.

Prick the pastry base with a fork and line with foil and baking beans. Bake in a preheated oven at 200°C (190°C fan oven)/gas 6 for 15 minutes. Remove the foil and beans, and bake for 5 minutes more. Remove from the oven and allow to cool.

Meanwhile, cut the medlars in half and spoon out the flesh, discarding the seeds. Push through a nylon sieve to remove any tough stringy bits. You will need about 350 g/12 oz of sieved flesh.

Put the flesh in a blender with the sugar, spices, salt, eggs and cream, and purée until smooth.

Pour the mixture into the pastry case. Bake in a preheated oven at 190°C (180°C fan oven)/gas 5 for 45–50 minutes or until a knife inserted in the centre comes out clean. Sprinkle with icing sugar.

Serve warm with ricotta cream, whipped cream or thick yogurt.

MEDLAR AND GINGER CREAMS

SERVES 4

Medlars are ready for eating in the late autumn when they have 'bletted': the flesh turns soft and brown, and the skins change from greenish-brown to a darker brown. The pleasantly sharp flesh is certainly an acquired taste, but is delicious mixed with cream and spices. Serve with Langues de Chat biscuits.

600 g / 1¼ lb bletted medlars
1½ tbsp finely chopped stem ginger
4 tbsp ginger syrup from the jar
175 ml / 6 fl oz apple juice
1½ tbsp lemon juice
125 ml / 4 fl oz whipping cream, whipped
slivers of stem ginger, to decorate

Slice the medlars in half and spoon out the flesh, discarding the seeds. Push through a nylon sieve to remove any tough stringy bits. You will need about 225 g/8 oz of sieved flesh.

Mix the flesh with the ginger, syrup, apple juice and lemon juice.

Whip the cream until just firm. Swirl into the medlar mixture. Spoon into individual serving glasses and chill.

Decorate with one or two very thin slivers of stem ginger just before serving.

VARIATION
Replace the ginger and ginger syrup with 1½ tablespoons of acacia honey and 1 tsp ground cinnamon. Decorate with a drizzle of honey and a few thin slices of almonds with skin.

Desserts with Stone Fruit

Summer wouldn't be summer without mouthwatering stone fruit – fragrant apricots, plump peaches and nectarines, and later on, plums and greengages. When they first come into season it's madness to do anything other than eat these luscious treats just as they are, with the juices streaming down your fingers. But as the summer wears on and fruits become more plentiful, other ideas spring to mind.

You'll find recipes here for mousses, fools and cheesecakes – normally fat-laden concoctions which I've treated with a lighter touch. The proportion of fruit is increased so the flavour remains strong, and it's combined with creamy ricotta cheese, quark or smetana – all naturally low in fat and delicious, and a far cry from ridiculous concepts such as 'half-fat double cream'.

APRICOTS

A sun-warmed apricot picked at the peak of ripeness is sheer heaven, but a treat usually denied to most of us. With their soft velvety skins and delicate flesh, apricots do not travel well and more often than not are picked for export while under-ripe and still firm. The texture can sometimes be mealy, instead of glisteningly translucent. The skins are deceptive too – a sunny mixture of pink, yellow and orange is not necessarily a guarantee of flavour. But you can be lucky if you buy your apricots from a reliable source. Fortunately, a light poaching in a scented syrup will rescue less-than-perfect fruit, or they can be puréed with a little sugar and lemon juice for use in ices and fools.

The skins quickly wrinkle if you leave apricots in the fruit bowl for too long. Eat them within a few days or store in a plastic box in the fridge.

Both fresh and dried apricots are packed with nutrients – amazingly high levels of carotene (vitamin A) and potassium, with good amounts of fibre, carbohydrate, folate (one of the B vitamins) and vitamin C.

Source	Season
France	June–August
Greece	May–July
Italy	June–August
Spain	May–July
Turkey	May–July

PEACHES AND NECTARINES

With their soft fuzzy skin and succulent flesh, peaches must be the most sensual of all fruit, with nectarines coming a close second. Edward Bunyard, in his wonderful *The Anatomy of Dessert* (1929), charmingly describes the smooth-skinned nec-tarine as 'a peach which has lost its *duvet*'. Both fruits have white, pink or yellow flesh, and are classified as free-stone or cling-stone, depending on whether or not the flesh clings to the stone. White-fleshed fruit are the sweetest of all.

As with apricots, quality suffers if peaches and nectarines are picked too soon, so buy them from a reputable greengrocer or supermarket known for selling fruit at the point of ripeness.

The slightest bruising will cause the fruit to deteriorate rapidly. Choose those with unblemished skins and firm flesh, and eat them within a few days, before the flavour has a chance to escape.

Peaches and nectarines are a good source of fibre, carbohydrate, potassium and vitamin C.

Source	Season
France	June–October
Italy	June–September
Spain	May–September
United States	May–September

CHERRIES

Available all year round, cherries are expensive, perhaps only worth buying during the summer when prices are more reasonable.

There are two types of cherry: sweet and sour. Ripe cherries have beautifully plump juicy flesh and an intense flavour which is both sweet and sharp. They're best eaten raw in my opinion. The skin of ripe cherries may be a deep ruby red, black, or white or yellow streaked with red.

Sour cherries include Morello and Montmorency. Dried Montmorency cherries must be my favourite snack – they have a wonderfully tart complex flavour which makes the tongue tingle. Adding a few to a dessert made with fresh cherries really brings out the essential taste. You can buy them in the better supermarkets, but unfortunately they are an expensive and addictive habit.

When buying fresh cherries look for tender green stems – brittle brown stems are a sign that they are past their best – and avoid fruit that is bruised or split. They are best eaten within a day or two of buying, but will keep in the fridge for up to a week. A cherry stoner is invaluable for preparing them.

Cherries contain useful amounts of most nutrients, as well as a substance known as ellagic acid, thought to fight cancer by blocking an enzyme used by cancer cells.

Source	Season
France	May–July
Italy	June–July
South Africa	October–December
United Kingdom	June–August
United States	May–August

PLUMS

Considering the number of fascinating varieties of these late summer fruit, the supermarkets offer us a poor choice, consisting mainly of Victorias, Stanleys, Santa Rosas, rock-hard greengages, and damsons if you're lucky. You will have to search hard for Coe's Golden Drop, Esperen or Warwickshire Droopers. Local markets, specialist fruit farms or private gardens are your best bet.

Plums can be loosely divided into cooking, and dessert or eating varieties. As with peaches, there are free-stones and clings. The skins range from golden yellow to inky purple.

Of the cooking plums, the quetsch from Alsace in France is the best variety. Small, dark purple and intensely flavoured, it makes excellent tarts. Damsons are another strongly flavoured plum worth looking for. Use them in mousses, ice-creams and crumbles.

Dessert plums have a higher sugar content and a better flavour than cooking plums, and they can be used in cooking too. The best-known is the Victoria – oval, yellow or red-skinned, with a slightly bland, juicy flesh. Finest and sweetest of all must be the greengage, which is in fact an old variety of plum (the British are the only country to make a distinction between them). When fully ripe, the greenish-golden flesh is sweetly aromatic and succulent. Eat them raw or use in crumbles, ice-creams and compotes.

When choosing plums, look for unwrinkled specimens with a nice bloomy skin. Firm fruit can be kept for up to a week and will continue to ripen at room temperature. Putting them in a brown paper bag will speed up the process. A fully ripe plum will be slightly soft near the stalk, perhaps with a bead of sticky moisture on the skin. The peak of perfection is short-lived, so use right away.

Prunes are simply dried plums, but not all plums can become prunes. A successful prune needs a particularly sweet type of prune plum which can be dried without fermenting while still containing the stone. The best prunes are plump, moist and juicy and require no soaking. The giant black variety from Agen in France and Elvas in Portugal are particularly good. Prunes have an unfortunate reputation but with an inspired touch they make delicious healthy fruit desserts.

Plums provide useful amounts of potassium and carotene (vitamin A). Prunes contain copious amounts of pectin, a type of dietary fibre, which accounts for their laxative effect. They are rich in carbohydrate and potassium too, and contain good levels of calcium, magnesium, carotene (vitamin A), B group vitamins, and vitamins E and C.

Source	Season
France	July–October
Italy	July–October
South Africa	January–April
Spain	June–September
United Kingdom	August–October
United States	May–November

APRICOT AND SAFFRON CHEESECAKE

SERVES 8–10

A rich, creamy but low-fat cheesecake, with just a hint of saffron. It is made with uncooked egg white so should be kept well chilled and eaten within 24 hours. Dried apricots contain plenty of fibre, minerals and vitamins, particularly carotene (vitamin A).

1 Cheesecake Base (page 200)
175 g/6 oz dried apricots, preferably unsulphured
225 g/8 oz low-fat quark
225 ml/8 fl oz wholemilk organic yogurt
75 g/3 oz sugar
pinch of saffron threads
finely grated zest of 1 lemon
15 g/½ oz powdered gelatine
2 egg whites
toasted flaked almonds, to decorate

Lightly grease the base and sides of a 23 cm/9 inch springform tin. Press your chosen base mixture into the tin, and chill or bake according to the recipe.

Put the apricots in a small saucepan with enough water to cover. Bring to the boil, then simmer for 15–20 minutes until soft. Transfer to a food processor or blender and purée until smooth.

Beat together the quark, yogurt and sugar, then beat in the apricot purée.

Pound the saffron threads in a mortar and dissolve in 1 tablespoon of boiling water. Add to the apricot mixture along with the lemon zest.

Put 4 tablespoons of boiling water into a bowl. Sprinkle the gelatine over the surface and leave until spongy. Place over a pan of hot water until completely dissolved. Stir into the apricot mixture, mixing well.

Whisk the egg whites until stiff. Using a metal spoon, fold about one-third into the apricot mixture to slacken it, then gently fold in the rest.

Pour the mixture into the tin and chill for 4–5 hours or overnight. Carefully remove from the tin and decorate with almonds.

FROZEN APRICOT AND STRAWBERRY SAVARIN

SERVES 4

Dried apricots mixed with fresh apricot purée intensify the flavour and add agreeable nuggets of chewiness to the texture. Apricots, both fresh and dried, are a super healthfood. They're extremely rich in energy-giving carbohydrate, and carotene (vitamin A) – an antioxidant vitamin known to reduce the risk of cancer. Apricots also contain massive amounts of potassium and are a good source of calcium, magnesium, iron and zinc.

400 g / 14 oz ripe apricots
juice of 1 lemon
75 g / 3 oz sugar
50 g / 2 oz dried apricots, finely chopped
4 tbsp double cream
15 g / ½ oz flaked almonds, toasted until golden
150 g / 5 oz small strawberries
Strawberry Syrup (page 214), to serve

Cut the fresh apricots in half and scoop out the stones. Chop the flesh roughly.

Put the fresh apricots, lemon juice and sugar in a blender. Purée until smooth, then stir in the dried apricots and cream.

Pour the mixture into a shallow freezerproof container. Cover the surface with clingfilm, then freeze for about 2 hours until hard round the edges.

Transfer to a mixing bowl and whisk until smooth. Repeat once more if you have time.

Lightly grease, or line with clingfilm, a 600 ml (1 pint) ring mould. Put in the freezer to chill.

Spoon the whisked apricot mixture into the prepared

mould. Smooth the surface, cover with clingfilm and freeze until firm.

To unmould the savarin, leave to stand at room temperature for 20 minutes. Dip the mould in hot water for a few seconds. Wipe dry, then invert on to a serving plate. Remove the mould and smooth the surface with a wet knife.

Scatter with the almonds and pile the strawberries in the centre.

Pour a little strawberry syrup on to individual chilled plates, then add a serving of savarin and the strawberries.

CARAMELIZED APRICOTS WITH CARDAMOM AND LEMON

SERVES 6

I once made this with dried apricots which cooked to an almost toffee-like goo, partly because I left them in the oven for too long. Not wanting to see my efforts wasted, I tipped the whole lot into the blender and ended up with a delicious cardamom-scented jam which has since become a household favourite. Made with fresh apricots, this is a good way of using fruits which are a bit hard and lacking in flavour.

900 g / 2 lb apricots
4 tbsp water
100 g / 4 oz sugar
crushed seeds from 6 cardamom pods
finely grated zest of 1 lemon
shelled pistachio nuts, chopped, to decorate

Cut the apricots all round the indentation through to the stone. Twist the two halves in opposite directions, then scoop out the stone.

Arrange the apricots in a shallow ovenproof dish, cut side down and slightly overlapping.

Put the water, sugar, cardamom seeds and lemon zest in a small saucepan. Heat gently, stirring, until the sugar has dissolved, brushing down the sides of the pan with water to prevent sugar crystals forming.

Raise the heat and boil for 1–2 minutes until syrupy. Immediately remove from the heat.

Pour the syrup over the apricots. Bake in a preheated oven at 240°C (230°C fan oven)/gas 9 for 15–20 minutes until bubbling and the apricots are slightly blackened.

Allow to cool to room temperature. Decorate with pistachio nuts just before serving.

VARIATION

Replace the cardamom with a few small sprigs of rosemary, and use toasted pine kernels instead of pistachios. The flavours combine remarkably well.

APRICOTS, PRUNES AND WHEAT GRAINS IN LEMON SYRUP

SERVES 4

This is a useful winter dessert which is particularly delicious made with prunes bottled in Armagnac. You can buy wheat grains from healthfood shops. They have a pleasantly chewy texture and a mild flavour, and are a good accompaniment to both fruit and vegetables. Start the day before to allow time for overnight soaking. Eat soon after adding the syrup as the wheat will become tough if left to stand for too long. This dessert is packed with nutrients – protein, carbohydrate, fibre, minerals and vitamins, particularly carotene (vitamin A).

225 g/8 oz whole wheat grains, soaked overnight
100 g/4 oz dried apricots, halved and soaked overnight
50 g/2 oz prunes, soaked overnight
150 ml/¼ pint medium or heavy Sugar Syrup (page 210), made with finely grated lemon zest
whipped cream, Ricotta Cream (page 206) or Low-Fat Thick Cream (page 207), to serve
40 g/1½ oz flaked almonds, toasted

Drain the whole wheat grains and cook in plenty of boiling water for 1–1½ hours until very soft. Drain and allow to cool. Put in a serving bowl or individual bowls.

Drain the fruit and add to the wheat grains. Pour over the syrup, top with a blob of cream and sprinkle with the almonds.

SPICED FRUIT FOOL

SERVES 4–6

This is good for using up fruit that is slightly bruised, but it must be perfectly ripe with a good flavour. Pear juice concentrate is sold in good healthfood shops, as are dried coconut ribbons. The juice concentrate is a natural sweetener, so you won't need to add much extra sugar. This dessert contains some protein, as well as reasonable amounts of fibre, calcium, magnesium and vitamin C.

700 g / 1½ lb peaches, nectarines or apricots, or a mixture
juice of ½ lemon
3 tbsp pear juice concentrate
½ tsp ground cinnamon
½ tsp allspice berries, crushed
225 ml / 8 fl oz wholemilk organic yogurt
toasted coconut ribbons (page 219), to decorate
sugar, to taste

Quarter the fruit lengthways and remove the stones. Using a small sharp knife, cut away the skin and roughly chop the flesh. Purée in a food processor or blender with the lemon juice, pear juice concentrate and spices. The purée can be a little bit chunky if you like. You should have 500 ml / 18 fl oz.

Divide among individual glass serving bowls. Swirl in the yogurt then chill thoroughly. Sprinkle with the coconut ribbons just before serving. Add sugar to taste.

VARIATION
Instead of cinnamon and allspice, try the crushed seeds of 4–6 cardamom pods with a teaspoon of finely chopped stem ginger, and a little bit of syrup from the jar.

KHOSHAF

SERVES 3–4

The classic version of this wonderful Middle Eastern fruit salad contains only apricots and raisins, but you could add prunes as I have done, or replace some of the apricots with dried apple rings, pears or peaches. Pomegranate seeds are another good addition. You need to begin preparation at least a day in advance to allow for soaking time. Dried apricots are rich in carotene (vitamin A) and fibre. The natural sweetness of the orange juice and fruit means you don't need to add much sugar.

3 large oranges
225 g/8 oz dried apricots or other dried fruit
50 g/2 oz prunes
50 g/2 oz raisins
sugar, to taste
2 tsp orangeflower water
25 g/1 oz almonds with skin, halved lengthways
15 g/½ oz shelled pistachio nuts
15 g/½ oz pine kernels
pomegranate seeds (optional)

Squeeze the oranges and pour the strained juice into a large bowl.

Cut the apricots into chunks and add to the orange juice with the prunes and raisins. Add enough water to cover the fruit. Stir in a little sugar to taste, bearing in mind that the fruit and the orange juice are naturally sweet. Sprinkle with the orangeflower water. Cover and leave to soak overnight or up to 2 days.

Remove the stones from the prunes and quarter the flesh lengthways.

Add the nuts and the pomegranate seeds, if using. Serve slightly chilled.

PEACHES WITH GREEN PEPPERCORNS AND MINT

SERVES 4

Green peppercorns have a mysterious smoky flavour which is magical combined with peaches. This is an effective rescue remedy for peaches that are a bit hard and flavourless.

6 peaches
1–2 tbsp lime juice
100 g / 4 oz sugar
150 ml / ¼ pint water
1 tbsp dried green peppercorns
1 tbsp shredded fresh mint

Cut the peaches round the indentation though to the stone. Twist the two halves sharply in opposite directions to loosen the stone, then scoop it out with a knife.

Peel off the skin with a small sharp knife, taking care not to damage the flesh.

Slice the flesh lengthways into segments and put in a serving bowl. Sprinkle with the lime juice to prevent discoloration.

Put the sugar, water and peppercorns in a small saucepan. Stir over a low heat until the sugar has dissolved. Raise the heat and boil hard for 5–10 minutes until syrupy.

If the peaches are on the hard side, immediately strain the hot syrup over them, reserving the peppercorns. If the peaches are soft, allow the syrup to cool a little before adding it.

Stir in the mint. Sprinkle with a few of the reserved peppercorns, bearing in mind that not everybody likes to chew on whole spices. Leave to cool completely before serving. Serve at room temperature.

PEACH AND AMARETTI RICOTTA ICE-CREAM

SERVES 8

Ricotta reduces the fat content of the ice-cream without compromising on creaminess. Use top quality perfectly ripe peaches with a strong flavour.

800 g / 1¾ lb peaches
3 tbsp lemon juice
100 g / 4 oz sugar
2 tbsp amaretto liqueur (optional)
200 g / 7 oz ricotta
150 ml / ¼ pint whipping cream
40 g / 1½ oz amaretti biscuits
peach slices, to decorate
whole amaretti biscuits, to serve

Halve the peaches and scoop out the stones. Cut in half again and remove the skin with a sharp knife. As you work, sprinkle with some of the lemon juice to prevent discoloration.

Finely chop the flesh of two of the peaches, sprinkle with more lemon juice, cover and set aside.

Roughly chop the remaining peaches. Put in a food processor or blender with the sugar and remaining lemon juice. Purée until smooth, then transfer to a mixing bowl. Stir in the liqueur, if using.

Mix the ricotta and cream until smooth, then fold into the peach mixture. Pour into a shallow freezer-proof container. Cover the surface with clingfilm and freeze for about 2 hours until hard round the edges.

Transfer the mixture to a mixing bowl and whisk until smooth. Freeze and whisk again.

Put the amaretti biscuits in a plastic bag and bash lightly with a rolling pin to make large coarse crumbs (don't pound to a dust). Fold the crumbs into the peach mixture, together with the reserved chopped peaches. Freeze for several hours until completely firm.

Thirty minutes before serving, put in the fridge to soften. Decorate each serving with peach slices and serve with amaretti biscuits.

NECTARINE MOUSSE WITH PINEAPPLE SAGE

SERVES 4

A delicately flavoured mousse which looks beautiful served in tall glasses. Try it with lemon balm or fresh angelica if you don't have any pineapple sage. Ricotta cheese mixed with yogurt is a low-calorie alternative to whipped cream — and just as creamy. The recipe contains uncooked egg white and should be chilled and eaten within 24 hours.

5 very sweet ripe nectarines
lemon juice
2 tbsp low-fat yogurt
175 g / 6 oz ricotta cheese
sugar, to taste (optional)
150 ml / ¼ pint orange juice
small handful of fresh pineapple sage leaves, shredded
1 sachet powdered gelatine
2 egg whites
small fresh pineapple sage leaves, to decorate

Set aside half of one nectarine for decoration, sprinkling the cut surface with lemon juice to prevent discoloration.

Roughly chop the remaining nectarines, then put them in a food processor or blender with the yogurt and ricotta. Purée until smooth. Check for sweetness, adding a little sugar if necessary. Transfer the mixture to a large bowl.

Put the orange juice and pineapple sage in a small bowl. Sprinkle the surface with the gelatine and leave for 10 minutes until spongy. Heat over a pan of hot water until the gelatine has fully dissolved. Whisk into the nectarine mixture.

Whisk the egg whites until stiff. Fold about one-third into

the nectarine mixture to slacken it, then carefully fold in the rest.

Pour the mixture into individual serving glasses and chill for 2 hours until set.

When ready to serve, decorate each mousse with a tiny sprig of pineapple sage and thinly sliced segments of the remaining nectarine.

PEACHES IN STRAWBERRY ROSE SYRUP

SERVES 6

A mixture of white- and yellow-fleshed peaches, or peaches and nectarines, looks beautiful with the pink syrup. Use perfectly ripe fruit with no bruises. For a truly summery presentation, serve in a glass bowl placed on a plate and surrounded with scented pink rose petals.

9 large peaches
lemon juice
Strawberry Syrup (page 214)
¼–½ tsp rose water
fresh raspberries, to decorate

Peel the peaches by plunging into boiling water for 10 seconds, then drain and slip off the skins. (Sometimes there is no need to do this if the skin comes away easily by itself.)

Taking care not to bruise the flesh, cut the peaches in half lengthways and scoop out the stones. Cut each half into 3 segments. Sprinkle with a little lemon juice as you work, to prevent discoloration.

Put the peach slices in a glass serving bowl and pour over enough strawberry syrup to cover. Sprinkle with the rose water, then chill for 1 hour.

Decorate with fresh raspberries just before serving.

YOGURT ICE WITH FRESH AND DRIED CHERRIES

SERVES 6

Dried Montmorency cherries have an astringent, deeply intense flavour. You can buy them in large supermarkets. Mixing the cherries with yogurt instead of the usual egg yolk- and cream-based custard significantly lowers the fat content without any loss of richness. Serve with crisp biscuits such as amaretti or Langues de Chat.

600 g / 1¼ lb cherries
75 g / 3 oz dried Montmorency cherries
175 g / 6 oz sugar
1–2 tbsp kirsch or brandy (optional)
225 ml / 8 fl oz Greek yogurt

Set aside 12 whole cherries to decorate. Remove the stones from the remaining cherries, then put them in a blender with the dried cherries and sugar. Purée until smooth.

Add the kirsch or brandy, if using, then fold in the yogurt.

Pour the mixture into a shallow freezerproof container. Cover the surface with clingfilm. Freeze for about 2 hours until beginning to harden around the edges.

Transfer to a mixing bowl and whisk until smooth. Freeze again. Repeat the process twice more if you have time, then freeze until completely firm.

Decorate each serving with the reserved cherries.

CHERRY PANCAKES

SERVES 4

Try flavouring the batter with a little kirsch. You can use either the normal batter (page 202) or eggless batter (page 204). Keep the pancakes warm in a low oven while you make the filling.

1 kg/2 lb 4 oz cherries, pitted
4 tbsp sugar
juice of 1 lemon
1 tsp ground cinnamon
½ tsp cornflour
8 pancakes
chopped walnuts, to decorate
sieved icing sugar, for dusting

Purée 225 g/8 oz of the cherries in a blender for 2–3 minutes until very smooth.

Put the cherry purée in a saucepan with the sugar, lemon juice, cinnamon and the rest of the cherries. Bring to the boil, then simmer for 3–5 minutes until the cherries are just tender but still hold their shape.

Strain the cherries, reserving the syrup, and put in a bowl.

Mix the cornflour to a smooth paste with 1 tablespoon of water. Return the syrup to the pan and add the cornflour. Stir over a gentle heat for about 3 minutes until thickened. Set aside and keep warm.

Fold the pancakes into cones and fill with the cherries. Arrange in a shallow ovenproof dish and reheat in a preheated moderate oven for 10 minutes.

Sprinkle with walnuts and dust with icing sugar. Serve the cherry sauce in a jug.

PLUM COMPOTE WITH ORANGE ZEST AND ROSEMARY

SERVES 6

There is a particular type of plum compote that I really dislike – it must be something to do with memories of school dinners. The plum skins are tough and sour, while the flesh disintegrates into a watery, tasteless syrup. However, barely cooked plums in a rosemary-scented syrup are another matter entirely. This works best with those imported black-skinned plums with a firm flesh, often sold by supermarkets in the winter. The syrup is absolutely delicious – the flavour of rosemary and orange will have your friends guessing.

900 g/2 lb dark-skinned plums
600 ml/1 pint water
200 g/7 oz sugar
finely grated zest of 1 orange
2 large fresh rosemary sprigs
40 g/1½ oz almonds with skin

Cut the plums all the way round the indentation through to the stone. Sharply twist the two halves in opposite directions to loosen the stone, then scoop it out. Cut the flesh lengthways into segments and put in a serving bowl.

Put the water, sugar, orange zest and rosemary in a saucepan. Heat gently until the sugar has dissolved. Raise the heat and boil for 7–10 minutes.

Immediately strain the boiling syrup over the plums. The heat will cook the plums just enough to make them palatable without turning them into a slop. Leave to cool to room temperature.

Slice the almonds lengthways into slivers and add to the plums just before serving.

SALAD OF DARK FRUITS IN SPICED SYRUP

SERVES 6

A dramatic salad with an enigmatic flavour, best served at room temperature. The redcurrants look like tiny gleaming jewels scattered over the rich dark purples and reds of the cherries, plums and nectarines.

600 g / 1¼ lb mixed dark-skinned stone fruit, such as nectarines, plums, cherries
100 g / 4 oz seedless red grapes
225 g / 8 oz mixed dark soft fruit, such as blueberries, raspberries, mulberries
50 g / 2 oz redcurrants

SPICED SYRUP
300 ml / ½ pint water
100 g / 4 oz sugar
small strip of thinly pared orange peel
2 fresh rosemary sprigs
2 thin slices of fresh ginger root
8 black peppercorns, crushed
8 coriander seeds, crushed
2.5 cm / 1 inch cinnamon stick

Prepare the stone fruit. Cut the nectarines and plums in half, twist the two halves in opposite directions to loosen the stone, then scoop it out. Slice the flesh lengthways into segments, then cut each segment in half crossways. Remove the cherry stones. Put in a serving bowl with the grapes.

Put all the syrup ingredients in a small saucepan. Stir over a gentle heat until the sugar has dissolved. Raise the heat and boil for 7–10 minutes.

Strain the syrup and allow to cool a little. Pour over the fruit in the bowl and leave to cool completely.

Just before serving, add the soft fruit and scatter the redcurrants over the top.

PLUM AND AMARETTI CRUNCH

SERVES 4

This looks and tastes like a very creamy high-fat dessert, but combining ricotta cheese and yogurt with a small amount of whipped cream considerably reduces the fat content.

350 g / 12 oz dark-skinned plums
100 g / 4 oz sugar
300 ml / ½ pint water
12.5 cm / 5 inch cinnamon stick
2 thinly pared strips orange peel
150 ml / ¼ pint whipping cream
150 g / 5 oz ricotta cheese
150 ml / ¼ pint Greek yogurt
40 g / 1½ oz amaretti biscuits, crumbled

Cut the plums all the way round the indentation through to the stone. Twist the two halves in opposite directions to loosen the stone, then scoop it out. Cut each half lengthways into thin segments.

Put the sugar and water in a small saucepan with the cinnamon and orange peel. Stir over a medium heat until the sugar has dissolved. Add the plums, bring to the boil, then simmer for about 3 minutes – just long enough to soften them but without losing their shape.

Drain the plums and return the juice to the pan. Boil for 5–8 minutes until syrupy, then allow to cool.

Whip the cream in a large bowl until stiff. Beat in the ricotta and yogurt, then fold in the plums. Divide the mixture among 4 individual serving glasses, or pour into one large serving bowl, then cover and chill.

Just before serving, stir in the crumbled amaretti, and swirl in enough of the syrup to sweeten.

GREENGAGE AND PISTACHIO CRUMBLE

SERVES 6

Crumbles are one of those homely desserts which never fail to please. Serve this with Vanilla Custard (page 209), Buttermilk Sauce (page 207) or creamy wholemilk organic yogurt.

700 g / 1½ lb ripe greengages
100 g / 4 oz sugar
90 g / 3½ oz butter
50 g / 2 oz shelled pistachio nuts
100 g / 4 oz plain flour
50 g / 2 oz rolled oats
demerara sugar, for dusting

Cut the greengages all the way round the indentation through to the stone. Separate the two halves by twisting in opposite directions, then scoop out the stone.

Put the greengages in a saucepan with 3 tablespoons of the sugar and 15 g / ½ oz of the butter. Cook over a medium heat for about 5 minutes until the juices start to flow, then tip into a 1 L / 1¾ pint pie dish.

Cover the pistachios with boiling water, leave for 5 minutes, then drain and slip off the skins. Chop the nuts fairly finely.

Sift the flour into a bowl and stir in the oats. Rub in the remaining butter until the mixture resembles coarse bread-crumbs, then stir in the pistachio nuts and the remaining sugar. Add 1 tablespoon of water and mix to a crumbly dough.

Scatter the crumble over the greengages, then dust with demerara sugar.

Bake in a preheated oven at 200°C (190°C fan oven)/gas 6 for 35–40 minutes until the crumble is crisp and golden.

YOGURT CHEESE WITH HOT PRUNE AND RAISIN SAUCE

SERVES 6

The hot, richly flavoured sauce makes a perfect contrast to chilled creamy cheese. You could use ordinary ricotta if you don't have time to make the cheese. The sauce would also be good with very cold home-made vanilla ice-cream. Look for giant black semi-dried French prunes from Agen – the quality is infinitely superior. Make the sauce the day before.

400 g/14 oz Yogurt Cheese (page 208)
1½ tbsp clear honey, or to taste
crushed seeds from 4 cardamom pods
3 tbsp flaked almonds, toasted

SAUCE
225 g/8 oz giant Agen prunes
50 g/2 oz raisins
12.5 cm/5 inch cinnamon stick
75 ml/3 fl oz port or red wine
1 tbsp sugar, or to taste
juice of ½ lemon

Beat the cheese with the honey and cardamom. Cover and leave in the fridge to chill.

Remove the stones from the prunes, then put them in a small casserole with the raisins, cinnamon and port or red wine, and enough water to cover. Cover tightly and cook in a preheated oven at 160°C (150°C fan oven)/gas 2 for about 2 hours, until the fruit is very soft and the liquid has thickened.

Put the fruit and its liquid in a blender with sugar to taste and the lemon juice, and purée until smooth. Set aside until ready to serve.

Mix the almonds with the cheese and put a small mound on chilled individual serving plates.

Gently reheat the sauce, taking care not to let it burn, and pour over the cheese. Serve at once.

PRUNE AND RAISIN SOUFFLÉ

SERVES 6

Prunes are loaded with valuable nutrients – carbohydrate, fibre, calcium and iron – so it's worth experimenting with different ways of using them. Here, a dark and intense purée is mixed with egg white and cooked to a fluffy soufflé. The purée could also be used as a tart filling – try it with Nut Pastry made with walnuts (page 193) – or mixed with yogurt and frozen, or served as a fool.

4 egg whites
1 quantity cold Prune and Raisin Sauce (facing page)

Whisk the egg whites in a large bowl until stiff. Fold about one-third into the sauce to slacken it, then carefully fold in the rest.

Pour the mixture into a 2 litre/3½ pint soufflé dish. Set it in a roasting tin of hot water and bake in a preheated oven at 150°C (140°C fan oven)/gas 2 for 45–55 minutes until firm. Serve at once. The soufflé will sink as it cools.

PRUNE AND WALNUT CHOCOLATE PUDDING

SERVES 4–5

This is an extremely unglamorous nursery pud which will have you clamouring for more. I've adapted it from a recipe which came with a packet of enormous sticky French prunes from Agen. Prunes as delicious as this should be a regular ingredient in healthy desserts. They're very rich in fibre, carbohydrate and potassium, and they're also a good source of calcium, magnesium and iron.

100 g / 4 oz sunflower margarine
75 g / 3 oz light muscovado sugar
1 egg (size 2)
100 g / 4 oz self-raising flour
100 g / 4 oz large no-soak prunes, pitted and roughly chopped
25 g / 1 oz walnuts, chopped

SAUCE
50 g / 2 oz light muscovado sugar
25 g / 1 oz unsweetened cocoa powder
300 ml / ½ pint hot water

Beat the margarine and sugar until creamy, then gradually beat in the egg. Fold in the flour, then the prunes and walnuts. Spoon the mixture into a lightly greased 1.5 L/2½ pint ovenproof dish, and level the surface.

Next, combine the sugar and cocoa powder for the sauce. Add the hot water and stir until smooth. Pour the mixture over the top of the pudding.

Bake in a preheated oven at 190°C (180°C fan oven)/gas 5 for 25–30 minutes.

Desserts with Berries

With few exceptions, berries are one of the dwindling number of truly seasonal fruits. Strawberries, raspberries and red- and blackcurrants are high-summer classics, blackberries tell me autumn is on its way, while cranberries spell Thanksgiving and Christmas. Seasonal markers are, I believe, essential for our well-being and good health. And there's no denying that all fruits and vegetables taste better when they are in their proper season.

When summer berries first appear, the simplest treatment is all that's required in most cases – nothing more than a light dusting of sugar – but as the novelty wears off you'll want to try other ideas.

This chapter gives recipes for old favourites and some new ideas too, always with an emphasis on freshness and lightness.

STRAWBERRIES

Something which passes for strawberries is available most of the year – a far cry from the deep colour and sweet, almost spicy flavour of a good-quality specimen. There are many varieties, shapes, and degrees of hairiness and pip. The most popular strawberry in Britain, and the one most widely available in supermarkets, is Elsanta, a fine-looking fruit with a succulent texture. But there are other discoveries to be made on pick-your-own farms. Sovereign, Rhapsody, Tenira and Red Gaunt-let are all delicious.

Look for firm, unblemished fruit with a fresh-looking calyx. Don't buy them if the punnet base is stained – the fruit at the bottom may be squashed or rotten. Strawberries are best eaten on the day of purchase, but will keep for a couple of days in the fridge if you store them with the calyx still attached.

If your strawberries need washing, do so very quickly and just before use. Remove the hulls afterwards, otherwise the fruit will become waterlogged. If you're picking your own strawberries, always do so by cutting the stems.

Strawberries have a very high vitamin C content – about a third more than oranges weight for weight – so eat them as often as you can. They contain ellagic acid, a substance thought to help fight cancer by blocking an enzyme used by cancer cells. Strawberries are also a good source of potassium and folate (one of the B vitamins), and they contain some iron too.

Source	Season
Belgium	April–September
France	May–October
Holland	April–October
Israel	November–April
Spain	February–June
United Kingdom	April–October

RASPBERRIES AND BLACKBERRIES

Best-known members of the bramble family, blackberries and velvety raspberries are a special summer treat. They are exquisite on their own with a light dusting of sugar and a blob of soft cream, or combined with other fruits – melons and peaches for instance, or in the classic summer pudding, or sprinkled over the top of a fruit salad.

Never buy raspberries with a stained punnet-base, and avoid

washing them – just check the insides for insect life and pick off the bits of stalk. It's essential to eat them on the day of purchase for they simply will not keep.

If you've gathered blackberries from the wild, you'll probably have to give them a lightning dip in water to get rid of dust and cobwebs. Lay them out on paper towel to dry, and handle very carefully for they are almost as perishable as raspberries.

Both raspberries and blackberries are rich in fibre and contain comparatively high levels of calcium, magnesium, iron, folate (one of the B vitamins), and vitamins C and E. What could be a nicer healthy treat?

Source	Season
France	May–October
United Kingdom	June–October

BLUEBERRIES

Originally a wild fruit from the woodlands of North America and Canada, blueberries are now successfully cultivated in Britain. They have a beautiful bluish-black skin with a powdery bloom, and sweet bluish flesh. They are expensive, but a few will go a long way. Add them to fruit salads, ice-cream or yogurt. Lime or lemon juice helps bring out their delicate flavour.

Choose berries that are plump and fresh-looking. Unlike other soft berries, blueberries will keep for up to 2 weeks in the fridge as long as they are not damaged. You can also buy them dried, canned or frozen.

Blueberries are a useful source of fibre, potassium, B vitamins and, when eaten raw, vitamin C.

Source	Season
United Kingdom	April–October
United States	January–December

RED- AND BLACKCURRANTS

Beautiful to look at and eat, these marvellous soft berries have a unique, tart, slightly earthy flavour. Redcurrants remind me of glass beads – I love to decorate ices and jellies with perfect strings of them, sometimes frosted with egg white and sugar. Both types are essential for the classic summer pudding, and combine well with peaches and melons. They make exquisite sorbets and jellies too.

Look for firm, glossy fruit, rejecting punnets which show signs of mould or stains. You can store them uncovered in the fridge for a day or two.

Both red- and blackcurrants are extremely rich in fibre and potassium, and contain comparatively high levels of calcium and iron. There is a wonderful comment about the nutritional benefits of blackcurrants in the excellent book *The Gardener and the Cook* by Lucy Yates (published 1912): 'While they are dyeing the lips of those who eat them they are enriching the blood'.

Weight for weight, blackcurrants contain about four times as much vitamin C as an orange. However, they must be cooked to make them palatable, and much of the vitamin will be destroyed by heat.

Source	Season
France	May–October
Holland	April–October
United Kingdom	July–August

GOOSEBERRIES

I have a suspicion that gooseberries, like medlars and quinces, could soon become a forgotten fruit. Gooseberries, too, are slightly weird, with their hairy skins and unique flavour; perhaps laziness over topping and tailing puts people off. I have included several recipes as a reminder of how delicious they are, especially when combined with elderflowers. Make the most of their short season which lasts from late May through to August.

The first gooseberries to appear are small, green and hard, and have the best flavour for cooking. They may be smooth-skinned or hairy. Later, you'll see large, deliciously sweet red varieties which can be eaten raw, or briefly cooked in a light fragrant syrup.

Choose firm fruit, rejecting any that are bruised or damaged. They keep well in the fridge – for 2–3 weeks if covered.

Gooseberries are a reasonable source of fibre, potassium and vitamin C.

Source	Season
Belgium	July
Holland	June–August
United Kingdom	June–August

CRANBERRIES

Cranberries are North America's only native berry. Known as 'rubies of the bogs', they grow on low bushes in fields which are artificially flooded at harvest-time. The berries are knocked off into the water, where they float to the collection point in a brilliant red wave. The harvest must be a magnificent sight.

I love their smooth, brilliant red skins and the way they bounce over the work surface. They need no topping and tailing, and are also very good-tempered about being stored. They will keep for weeks in the fridge as long as they are not damaged. Use them in sorbets, pies and cheesecakes, or add a few to a compote of autumn pears.

Cranberries contain useful levels of fibre, potassium, calcium and iron. They also contain small amounts of pycnogenol, a bioflavonoid which helps vitamin C to work effectively and protects the capillaries and skin. Some medical studies suggest that cranberry juice helps fight urinary tract infections too, by reducing levels of unwanted bacteria.

Source
United States

Season
October–January

STRAWBERRIES WITH SPICED SUGAR

SERVES 6

Strawberries with black pepper are a well-known combination, but this takes things a little further. Just savour the flavours! Strawberries are a useful ingredient in healthy desserts – they contain about one-third more vitamin C than oranges, and they're less messy to eat.

600 g / 1¼ lb large strawberries, unhulled
Spiced Sugar (page 211)

Briefly rinse the strawberries to get rid of any dust, then pat dry with paper towel.

Put the spiced sugar in a bowl in the centre of a large round serving plate. Scatter the strawberries round the edge. Let everybody help themselves, dipping the strawberries into the spice-scented sugar.

STRAWBERRY AND TARRAGON CUSTARDS

SERVES 6

Unlikely as it may sound, strawberries and tarragon are a happy combination. The warm, aniseedy scent of the tarragon infuses the custard with a subtle fragrance. A few lemon geranium leaves would be a delicious alternative.

450 ml/¾ pint semi-skimmed milk
6 large fresh tarragon sprigs
700 g/1½ lb strawberries
1 egg
2 egg yolks
50 g/2 oz caster sugar
3 tbsp lemon juice
1 sachet powdered gelatine
1 tbsp icing sugar
fresh strawberries, to decorate
fresh tarragon sprigs, to decorate

Put the milk in a saucepan with the tarragon sprigs. Bring to the boil, then remove from the heat. Cover and leave to infuse for 30 minutes before straining.

Purée the strawberries in a food processor or blender, roughly chopping them first if they are very large. Push the purée through a nylon sieve to get rid of any pips.

Whisk the whole egg and the yolks with the sugar. Add the strained milk and return to the pan. Simmer over a very low heat, stirring constantly, until the mixture just coats the back of a spoon. Do not overheat. Allow to cool.

Put the lemon juice in a small bowl. Sprinkle the gelatine over the surface and leave for 10 minutes until spongy. Place over a pan of hot water until the gelatine is completely dissolved. Stir into the custard, mixing well.

Whisk about two-thirds of the strawberry purée into the custard. Pour into lightly greased 150 ml/¼ pint ramekins and chill for 2–3 hours until set.

Whisk the icing sugar into the remaining purée.

To serve, run the tip of a knife around the edge of the ramekins and turn out the custards. Surround with the strawberry sauce and decorate with strawberries and tarragon sprigs.

STRAWBERRIES WITH ORANGE ZEST AND EAU DE COLOGNE MINT

SERVES 6

The first perfect berries of the summer need no tampering with apart from a dusting of caster sugar and some softly whipped cream. However, as the novelty wears off, you might want to experiment with other ways of preparing them. This is ideal for strawberries that are not as sweet as they might be. The combination with orange zest really intensifies the flavour, while the mint adds a refreshing touch.

600 g / 1¼ lb strawberries
3–4 sugar lumps
1 large orange, preferably unwaxed
tiny fresh Eau de Cologne mint sprigs

Slice the strawberries if they are very large and put them in a serving bowl.

Rub the sugar lumps over the orange skin until they are impregnated with the oil. Crumble over the strawberries and mix carefully.

Scatter with mint sprigs, then cover with clingfilm and leave to stand at room temperature for an hour or two to allow the flavours to mingle.

STRAWBERRY PIGNOLIA

SERVES 2–3

A combination of strawberries and *pignoli* (pine kernels) makes an energy-boosting dessert packed with carbohydrate, fibre, potassium, magnesium, folate and vitamin C. The dessert is said to be a favourite of the Seventh Day Adventists, who obviously like its health-promoting properties. It's also a good way of using up blemished strawberries.

65 g/2½ oz pine kernels
225 g/8 oz strawberries
1 tbsp clear honey, such as acacia or orange-blossom
3 bananas
2 tbsp lemon juice

Put the pine kernels on a baking sheet and toast for 3–5 minutes in a preheated moderate oven until golden. Be careful not to let them burn. Allow to cool.

Set aside a tablespoon of toasted pine kernels and 2–3 strawberries for decoration. Put the rest of the pine kernels and strawberries in a blender with the honey, bananas and lemon juice. Purée until smooth, then pour into individual serving bowls and chill.

Just before serving, sprinkle with the reserved chopped pine kernels and decorate with a strawberry.

FROZEN STRAWBERRY, BLUEBERRY AND NECTARINE TERRINE

SERVES 8

Start this a day and a half before you plan to serve it. Use perfectly ripe nectarines and strawberries with a good flavour. A nice touch is to flood each plate with a little Blueberry and Lime Syrup (page 212) or Strawberry Syrup (page 214), or chilled framboise eau de vie, before adding the terrine. Eat within a few days of making as the flavours deteriorate very rapidly.

8 tbsp clear mild-flavoured honey, such as acacia or orange blossom
300 ml / ½ pint fresh orange juice
4 tbsp lime juice
3 tbsp lemon juice
500 g / 1 lb 2 oz nectarines
250 g / 9 oz strawberries
250 g / 9 oz blueberries
nectarine slices, strawberries and blueberries, to decorate

Combine the honey, orange and lime juices in a measuring jug, mixing well until the honey is completely dissolved.

Cut the nectarines in half and scoop out the stones. Cut in half again and remove the peel with a sharp knife. As you work, sprinkle the flesh with some of the lemon juice to prevent discoloration.

Roughly chop the nectarine flesh and put in a blender. Purée with one-third of the honey mixture. Pour into a shallow freezerproof container and cover with clingfilm.

Purée the strawberries with another third of the honey mixture and the remaining lemon juice. Pour into a separate shallow freezerproof container and cover with clingfilm.

Finally purée the blueberries with the remaining honey mixture. Push through a fine sieve to get rid of pips. Pour into another freezerproof container and cover.

Freeze the 3 mixtures for 1–2 hours until firm around the edges. Beat until smooth to get rid of any ice crystals, return to the containers, cover and freeze again. Repeat the process once more if you have time, then freeze until completely solid.

Line a 1.3 L/2½ pint loaf tin with clingfilm. Remove the nectarine sorbet from the freezer and allow to soften slightly. Press it into the loaf tin, levelling the surface with a spatula. Refreeze until firm.

Repeat the layering and freezing, next with the strawberry sorbet, then with the blueberry sorbet, to make three layers. Cover and freeze for several hours until firm.

Thirty minutes before serving, put in the fridge to soften. When ready to serve, turn out on to a cutting board and remove the clingfilm. If the terrine refuses to budge from the tin, cover with a tea towel wrung out in hot water.

Using a knife dipped in hot water, cut into slices. Serve on chilled dessert plates and decorate with peach slices, strawberries and blueberries.

BLACKCURRANT AND CASSIS GRANITA

SERVES 4–6

A granita has a refreshing crunchy texture rather like snow. Stir it carefully with a fork when semi-frozen so as not to break up the ice crystals. Blackcurrants are extremely rich in vitamin C and are a good source of potassium, calcium and iron.

450 g / 1 lb blackcurrants
150 g / 5 oz sugar
450 ml / ¾ pint water
2 tbsp cassis
thin slices of nectarine, to decorate
fresh mint sprigs, to decorate

Put the blackcurrants in a small saucepan with 3–4 tablespoons of water. Cover and simmer for about 10 minutes until softened. Purée in a food processor or blender, then push through a fine nylon sieve to remove the pips.

Dissolve the sugar in the water over a medium heat, then boil for 5 minutes until syrupy. Remove from the heat and leave to cool.

Stir the blackcurrant purée into the syrup, with the cassis.

Pour the mixture into a shallow freezerproof container and freeze until beginning to harden round the edges. Stir the crystals from around the edge into the centre several times, but do not break them up – the mixture should be coarse and crunchy.

When ready to serve, remove from the freezer and scrape the surface of the granita with a fork to remove any large flaky crystals. Serve in tall individual serving glasses topped with nectarine slices and mint sprigs.

MIDNIGHT JELLY

SERVES 6

A very intense, grown-up jelly which encapsulates the essence
of blackcurrants. Blackcurrants contain extremely high levels
of vitamin C. Even though some of the vitamin will be
destroyed by cooking, a serving of jelly will provide you with
over three times the recommended daily amount. If you want
to cut down on the amount of sugar, try using fructose (fruit
sugar) instead – you'll need about 100 g/4 oz.

450 g / 1 lb blackcurrants, stalks removed
175 g / 6 oz sugar
1–2 tbsp cassis (optional)
2 tbsp powdered gelatine
redcurrants, to decorate
Ricotta Cream (page 206) or whipped cream, to serve

Put the blackcurrants and sugar in a saucepan. Heat slowly,
stirring, for 5 minutes until softened and the juices are flowing.
Purée in a blender, then push through a fine nylon sieve to
remove the pips.

Add the cassis, if using, and enough water to make the
mixture up to 900 ml/1½ pints.

Put 6 tablespoons of water in a small bowl and sprinkle the
gelatine over the surface. Leave for 10 minutes until spongy,
then heat over a pan of hot water until completely dissolved.

Add the gelatine to the blackcurrant mixture, mixing
thoroughly. Pour into a wetted mould, or individual moulds,
then cover and chill for several hours until set.

To turn out, run the tip of a knife round the edge of the
mould and dip the mould briefly into hot water. Invert over a
plate. Decorate with sprays of redcurrants and serve with a blob
of cream.

RASPBERRY, BLACKCURRANT AND REDCURRANT CONDÉ

SERVES 4

A classic dessert of very creamy, lightly spiced rice and vibrant berries. You can use arborio (Italian risotto) rice, or Thai fragrant, which I prefer because it has a softer texture.

250 g/9 oz raspberries
150 g/5 oz redcurrants, stalks removed
50 g/2 oz blackcurrants, stalks removed
2 tbsp sugar
1 tbsp cassis or raspberry liqueur (optional)

RICE
150 g/5 oz arborio or Thai fragrant rice
450 ml/¾ pint semi-skimmed milk
1 tbsp sugar
1 vanilla pod, split lengthways, or 1 tsp vanilla essence
1 cinnamon stick
150 ml/¼ pint low-fat organic yogurt
2 tbsp clear honey

Put the rice in a heavy-based saucepan with the milk, sugar and spices. Bring to the boil, then reduce to a gentle simmer for 20–30 minutes until tender and most of the milk has been absorbed. Remove the vanilla and cinnamon, and allow to cool.

Reserve some of the raspberries and redcurrants for decoration. Put the remaining redcurrants in a saucepan with the blackcurrants, sugar, and 1 tablespoon of liqueur, if using, or water. Bring slowly to the boil. Simmer until the skins have burst, then add the raspberries and simmer for another minute.

Some of the fruit should still hold its shape. Remove from the heat and leave to cool.

Stir the yogurt and honey into the cooled rice, then spoon into tall glasses with alternate layers of fruit. Decorate with the reserved raspberries and redcurrants and chill before serving.

SUMMER FRUIT BRIOCHE PUDDINGS

SERVES 6

This is a variation on the classic summer pudding and less fiddly to make. Cubes of day-old brioche are saturated with a purée of mixed berries, and pressed into individual ramekins. Toss the bread and fruit purée in a large bowl so that it is well mixed and all the liquid absorbed.

700 g / 1½ lb mixed summer fruits, such as strawberries, redcurrants, raspberries, pitted cherries and blackcurrants
2 tbsp sugar
175 g / 6 oz stale crustless brioche or challah bread, cut into
1 cm / ½ inch cubes
Ricotta Cream (page 206) or crème fraîche, to serve

Set aside 225 g/8 oz of whole fruits. Purée the remaining fruit with the sugar in a food processor or blender. Taste, and add more sugar if necessary – the mixture should be quite tart.

Pour the mixture into a large bowl. Toss in the bread cubes, turning until well mixed. Leave to stand until all the liquid is absorbed, tossing every so often.

Divide the mixture among six 150 ml/¼ pint ramekins. Press down with the back of a spoon. Cover the surface with clingfilm, allowing it to hang over the side. Weight each one down with cans or small weights. Chill for at least 4 hours or overnight.

To serve, run a knife round the edge of the ramekins and invert on to individual serving plates. Add the reserved whole fruit and a blob of cream.

RASPBERRY AND ELDERFLOWER SORBET

SERVES 4

Along with redcurrants, raspberries make the best sorbet of all. Elderflower syrup adds a subtle floweriness. Raspberries are comparatively rich in folate (one of the B vitamins), and are a good source of vitamin C.

400 g / 14 oz raspberries
3 tbsp lemon juice
100 g / 4 oz icing sugar
3 tbsp elderflower syrup
5 tbsp water
fresh raspberries, to decorate
fresh mint sprigs, to decorate

Purée the raspberries in a food processor or blender, then push the pulp through a fine sieve, pressing it with the back of a wooden spoon.

Stir the lemon juice and sugar into the purée, mixing well. Stir in the elderflower syrup and water.

Freeze in an ice-cream maker, following the manufacturer's instructions, or spoon the mixture into a shallow freezerproof container. Level with a spatula, cover the surface with clingfilm and freeze for 2 hours until beginning to harden round the edges.

Transfer to a bowl and whisk until smooth. Repeat the freezing and whisking twice more, if you have time, then freeze until firm.

Serve in individual glass serving bowls and decorate with raspberries and mint sprigs.

BLACKBERRIES WITH SPICED RICOTTA AND YOGURT CHEESE

SERVES 2

For a romantic presentation, make the cheese in china heart-shaped moulds with drainage holes in the base. If you don't have time to make the cheese, use ready-made ricotta instead. You could serve this with a little thin cream if you like, or leave as it is.

3–4 sugar lumps
1 orange
175 g/6 oz blackberries
175 g/6 oz Ricotta and Yogurt Cheese (page 208)
Spiced Sugar (page 211)
scented geranium leaves, to decorate

Rub the sugar lumps over the orange skin until they are deeply impregnated with the oil. Mix with the blackberries, leave for 10 minutes, then crumble the softened sugar lumps and toss gently to mix.

Mix the cheese with a little spiced sugar to taste, or use plain caster sugar if you don't have spiced sugar prepared.

Mould the cheese into balls and place on individual serving plates. Add the blackberries and decorate with a scented geranium leaf.

BLACKBERRY BREAD AND BUTTER PUDDING

SERVES 4

There is something very satisfying about bread puddings. This one with blackberries is light but comforting.

6 × 1 cm / ½ inch slices from a large white loaf, crusts removed
50 g / 2 oz butter or low-fat spread
150 g / 5 oz blackberries
finely grated zest of 1 orange
40 g / 1 ½ oz sugar
2 eggs
600 ml / 1 pint semi-skimmed milk
1 tsp vanilla essence

Spread the bread with butter or low-fat spread. Cut into fingers, then arrange half of them in the bottom of a lightly greased 1.1 L / 2 pint ovenproof dish.

Sprinkle with the blackberries, orange zest and half the sugar.

Top with the remaining bread, spread side uppermost. Sprinkle with the remaining sugar.

Next, beat together the eggs, milk and vanilla essence. Pour this over the bread, and leave to stand for 30 minutes to allow the bread to absorb the liquid.

Bake in a preheated oven at 170°C (160°C fan oven)/gas 3 for 1 hour, until puffy and golden-brown. Serve warm.

BLACKBERRY BATTER PUDDING

SERVES 4–6

This easily made and especially delicious pudding is based on a Russian recipe. Smetana is a rich but low-fat type of soured cream which you can buy in good supermarkets. Blackberries are an extremely good source of fibre, calcium, magnesium, folate and vitamin C. They also contain vitamin E.

450 g / 1 lb blackberries
1–2 tbsp blackberry eau de vie or kirsch (optional)
3 tbsp caster sugar
2 eggs (size 2)
1 tbsp plain flour
300 ml / ½ pint smetana
a little extra sugar, for sprinkling

Tip the berries into a shallow baking dish and sprinkle with the liqueur, if using, and 2 tablespoons of the sugar.

Put the dish in the oven, preheated to 150°C (140°C fan oven)/gas 2, for 20–30 minutes until the berries are thoroughly heated through.

Meanwhile, beat together the eggs and remaining sugar, then beat in the flour and the smetana.

Pour the mixture over the berries, and return the dish to the oven.

Bake for 45–50 minutes until pale golden and firm to touch. Sprinkle with a little more sugar before serving.

MIXED BERRY KISSEL

SERVES 4

This is adapted from a traditional Danish dessert which is a cross between a soup and a jelly. It is very intense and delicious, and packed with vitamins and minerals. If you don't have fresh fruit, a bag of frozen mixed berries would be fine.

500 g / 1 lb 2 oz mixed red fruits, such as redcurrants, blackberries, raspberries, strawberries and pitted cherries
50 g / 2 oz sugar, or to taste
½ tsp ground cinnamon
100 ml / 3½ fl oz port
1 tbsp arrowroot, mixed to a smooth paste with a little water
smetana or crème fraîche, to serve
finely grated orange zest, to decorate

Set aside a few whole fruits for decoration. Put the remaining fruit in a saucepan with 4 tablespoons of water. Simmer for about 10 minutes until the juices are flowing freely. Pour the mixture into a blender and purée until smooth, then push through a fine nylon sieve to get rid of the pips.

Pour the purée back into the pan. Add the sugar, cinnamon, port and 300 ml / ½ pint of water. Stirring over a medium heat, bring slowly to the boil. As the mixture comes to the boil, add the arrowroot, stirring vigorously. Continuing to stir, simmer over a medium heat for a few minutes until the mixture clears and thickens.

Pour into individual serving bowls, leave to cool, then cover with clingfilm and chill for several hours.

When ready to serve, swirl in a spoonful of smetana or crème fraîche, sprinkle with a little orange zest and decorate with the whole reserved fruits.

REDCURRANT SORBET

SERVES 4

Redcurrants are one of the dwindling number of fruits that are truly seasonal. This sorbet is one of my favourites, and celebrates their brief appearance. Eat within a few days – after that the flavour will deteriorate.

450 g / 1 lb redcurrants, stalks removed
300 ml / ½ pint medium Sugar Syrup (page 210)
sprays of redcurrants, to decorate

Purée the redcurrants in a blender, then push through a nylon sieve, extracting as much juice as possible.

Stir in the cold sugar syrup, mixing thoroughly. Freeze in an ice-cream maker, following the manufacturer's instructions, or pour into a shallow freezerproof container. Cover the surface with clingfilm and freeze until the mixture starts to harden around the edges.

Tip into a large bowl and beat until smooth. Repeat the process once more, then freeze overnight until completely firm.

Put in the fridge to soften about 1 hour before serving. Scoop into tall individual serving glasses and decorate with a spray of redcurrants.

VARIATION
Redcurrant and Lavender Sorbet Try using Lavender Syrup (page 216) instead of ordinary sugar syrup. The flavour is mysterious – not unlike honey. Decorate with a lavender sprig to give your guests a clue.

REDCURRANT YOGURT ICE

SERVES 4–6

A vibrantly pink, creamy ice which captures the essence of redcurrants and looks superb decorated with blue borage flowers. Eat the ice within a few days before the flavour escapes. Redcurrants are not only wonderful to eat, they also contain high levels of potassium, calcium and vitamin C.

150 g/5 oz sugar
150 ml/¼ pint water
450 g/1 lb redcurrants, stalks removed
150 ml/¼ pint whipping cream
150 ml/¼ pint Greek yogurt
sprays of redcurrants, to decorate
borage flowers, to decorate

Put the sugar and water in a small saucepan. Stir over a medium heat until the sugar has dissolved, then boil for 3 minutes. Remove from the heat and leave until completely cool.

Purée the redcurrants in a blender, then push through a nylon sieve and discard the debris. Fold the purée into the cold syrup.

Whip the cream until it just holds its shape. Stir the yogurt into the cream, then fold into the redcurrant purée.

Pour into a shallow freezerproof container. Cover the surface with clingfilm and freeze until the mixture starts to harden around the edges.

Tip into a mixing bowl and beat until smooth. Repeat the process once more, if you have time, then freeze overnight until completely firm.

About 1 hour before serving, put in the fridge to soften. Scoop into individual glass serving bowls and decorate with sprays of redcurrants and borage flowers.

GOOSEBERRY AND OAT CRUMBLE

SERVES 6

This is a satisfying, homely pud. Angelica adds a subtle floweriness to the flavour and seems to reduce the amount of sugar required. If you haven't got any angelica, use a little bit more sugar, or add a dash of orange-flower water. Oats are thought to help reduce blood cholesterol levels, and gooseberries are a reasonable source of fibre, potassium and vitamin C.

900 g/2 lb green gooseberries, topped and tailed
2–3 fresh angelica sprigs and some chopped stalk
75 g/3 oz sugar, or to taste

TOPPING
175 g/6 oz wholemeal plain flour
50 g/2 oz rolled oats
100 g/4 oz sunflower margarine
1½ tbsp muscovado sugar
1½ tbsp sunflower seeds

Put the gooseberries, angelica and sugar in a 1.5 L/2½ pint ovenproof baking dish.

Combine the flour and oats in a bowl, then stir in the margarine with a fork and mix until the mixture resembles breadcrumbs. Stir in the sugar.

Spoon the mixture over the fruit, pressing lightly to flatten. Bake in a preheated oven at 190°C (180°C fan oven)/gas 5 for 35–40 minutes.

GOOSEBERRY AND ALMOND PUDDING

SERVES 6

This is a delicately flavoured sponge with a hint of aniseed, moistened with Orange and Bay Syrup (page 215). Serve with Vanilla Custard (page 209).

200 g/7 oz self-raising flour
50 g/2 oz ground almonds
2 tsp baking powder
pinch of salt
100 g/4 oz softened butter or half-fat spread
100 g/4 oz sugar, plus 1 tbsp
2 eggs (size 2)
1 tbsp milk
seeds from 6 whole star anise pods, crushed
350 g/12 oz gooseberries, topped and tailed
Orange and Bay Syrup (page 215)

Mix together the flour, almonds, baking powder and salt. Put in a food processor with the softened butter, 100 g/4 oz of the sugar, the eggs, milk and all but a pinch of the crushed star anise seeds. Process until well mixed.

Spread a thin layer of the mixture over the base of a lightly greased ovenproof baking dish. Bake in a preheated oven at 180°C (170°C fan oven)/gas 4 for 5 minutes until set.

Mix the gooseberries with the remaining star anise seeds and sugar, then spread over the base of the pudding. Spread the rest of the mixture on top, levelling the surface. Bake for another 40–50 minutes, until golden-brown.

Poke several holes in the surface with a cocktail stick, and pour over some orange and bay syrup. Serve warm.

GOOSEBERRY AND ELDERFLOWER SYLLABUB

SERVES 6

If you have access to elderflowers unpolluted by traffic fumes, add 2–3 creamy heads to the gooseberries in the pan, and reduce the amount of elderflower syrup accordingly. There is no need to top and tail the gooseberries as the stalks will be sieved out. This dessert contains uncooked egg whites and should be kept chilled and eaten within 24 hours. Syllabubs are traditionally made with cream, but combining cream with fromage frais reduces the fat content without any loss of richness. Serve with macaroons or small ratafia biscuits.

500 g/1 lb 2 oz gooseberries
150 g/5 oz sugar
4 tbsp elderflower syrup
finely grated zest of 1 lemon
1 tbsp lemon juice
150 ml/¼ pint double cream
100 g/4 oz fromage frais
2 egg whites (size 2)

Put the gooseberries in a heavy-based saucepan with 75 g/3 oz of the sugar and 2 tablespoons of water. Cover and simmer for about 8 minutes until all the skins have burst. Push through a nylon sieve and discard the debris.

Put the gooseberry purée in a bowl, stir in 2 tablespoons of the elderflower syrup, then leave until completely cool.

Mix together the remaining elderflower syrup and sugar with the lemon zest and juice.

Whip the cream in a large bowl until stiff, then beat in the fromage frais. Gradually beat in the elderflower solution.

Whisk the egg whites until stiff but not dry and fold them into the syllabub, then gently fold in the gooseberry purée.

Pour into large wine glasses, then cover with clingfilm and chill for at least 6 hours.

RED GOOSEBERRIES WITH ORANGE AND BAY SYRUP

SERVES 3

This is delicious made with plump red dessert gooseberries. Allow time for the berries to macerate in the hot fragrant syrup.

40 g / 1½ oz whole almonds with skin
450 g / 1 lb red dessert gooseberries
1 quantity Orange and Bay Syrup (page 215)

Toast the almonds in a preheated moderate oven for 5–7 minutes. Top and tail the gooseberries and put them in a serving bowl.

Pour the hot syrup over the gooseberries – you can strain it if you like, but I think the bay leaf and orange peel look beautiful with the ruby-red gooseberries.

Allow to cool, then add the almonds. Serve at room temperature.

CRANBERRY AND PORT SORBET

SERVES 6–8

A beautiful deep red sorbet – perfect after a heavy Christmas meal. Add the port during the final whisking, before the sorbet freezes solid. Cranberries are thought to combat cystitis and other urinary tract infections.

250 g/9 oz cranberries
450 ml/¾ pint water
225 g/8 oz sugar
6 tbsp ruby port
orange segments, to decorate
almonds with skin, sliced lengthways, to decorate

Put the cranberries and water in a small saucepan. Bring to the boil, then simmer gently for 10 minutes until the cranberries are soft.

Put the cranberries and their cooking liquid in a blender. Purée until smooth, then push the mixture through a nylon sieve.

Put the cranberry purée in a bowl and stir in the sugar until dissolved. Transfer the mixture to a freezerproof container and freeze for several hours, until beginning to harden around the edges.

Put the mixture in a deep bowl and whisk until smooth. If you have time, freeze the mixture again until hard around the edges, then whisk again. Add the port during the final whisking. Freeze overnight until solid.

Remove the sorbet from the freezer 30 minutes before serving.

To make orange segments, peel an orange with a sharp knife, removing the thin outer membrane. Slide the knife down both sides of each segment, between the flesh and the membrane, and pull out the segments.

Serve scoops of sorbet in individual glass serving bowls and decorate each with an orange segment and a few slivers of almond.

BAKED CRANBERRY CHEESECAKE

SERVES 8–10

A plum-coloured, beautifully light cheesecake – almost like a mousse. If you love cheesecake but have to watch your fat intake, then quark is your salvation. It's a cheese made from skimmed milk and contains only the merest trace of fat, compared with ordinary cream cheese which is nearly 50 per cent fat.

1 Cheesecake Base (page 200)
225 g/8 oz cranberries
225 g/8 oz quark
225 ml/8 fl oz low-fat yogurt
100 g/4 oz sugar
2 eggs (size 2), separated
40 g/1½ oz plain flour
sifted icing sugar, to dust

Grease and line the base and sides of a 23 cm/9 inch spring-form tin. Press your chosen base into the tin and chill or bake according to the recipe.

Put the cranberries in a small saucepan with just enough water to cover them without floating. Bring to the boil, then simmer over a low heat for 10 minutes, until soft and thick.

Purée the cranberry mixture in a blender until smooth, then push through a nylon sieve.

Beat together the quark, yogurt and sugar in a large bowl. Beat in the cranberry purée, followed by the egg yolks and flour.

Whisk the egg whites until stiff, then lightly fold them into the quark mixture, using a metal spoon.

Pour the mixture into the tin and level the surface. Bake in a preheated oven at 170°C (160°C fan oven)/gas 3 for 1–1¼ hours, until a knife inserted in the centre comes out clean. Put a piece of foil over the top if it starts to look burnt.

Allow the cheesecake to cool in the tin – it will sink while doing so. Undo the tin and carefully peel away the paper. Dust with sifted icing sugar before serving.

CRANBERRY AND APRICOT TART

SERVES 6–8

There's something special about cranberries – their clear bright red skin reminds me of paste jewels from the dressing up box. They can be used in so many different ways, you can keep them in the fridge for ages before they start to deteriorate, and they don't need topping and tailing – so make the most of their short season. Serve the tart hot, warm or cold with Vanilla Custard (page 209) or Low-fat Thick Cream (page 207).

1 quantity All-In-One Shortcrust Pastry (page 192)
beaten egg white, for brushing
350 g / 12 oz cranberries, coarsely chopped
100 g / 4 oz no-soak dried apricots, finely chopped
175 g / 6 oz sugar
3 tbsp water
2 tbsp cornflour

Roll out the pastry thinly and use to line a 23 cm/9 inch loose-bottomed flan tin, pushing the sides up well. Brush with egg white and chill for 30 minutes.

Combine the cranberries and apricots. Mix in the sugar, water and cornflour. Pour the mixture into the pastry case.

Bake in a preheated oven at 230°C (220°C fan oven)/gas 8 for 10 minutes, then reduce the temperature to 180°C (170°C fan oven)/gas 4 and bake for 40 minutes more.

Desserts with Citrus Fruit

With their high vitamin C content, citrus fruits are probably the mainstay of a healthy diet, but we rarely get excited about them. As somebody once remarked, they're rather like wallpaper: always there but rarely noticed. However, I would find it hard to manage without at least the tangy zest of citrus fruit, if not the whole fruit. I share the consternation of Sydney Smith, the English essayist, who wrote, 'My living in Yorkshire was so far out of the way, that it was actually twelve miles from a lemon.'

This chapter gives you plenty of ideas for healthy desserts made with citrus fruits. The fruit is mainly left raw to preserve the vitamin C content, but I have indulged in one hot suety comfort pudding.

ORANGES, LOOSE-SKINNED CITRUS AND KUMQUATS

The original Jaffa orange is the shamouti – large, oval, with a thick, easy-peel skin and sweet flesh. Navels are another type of Jaffa, recognizable by the protrusion at one end. They are seedless and deliciously sweet. Valencia Lates appear at the end of the season. They too are very sweet and have few pips. Blood oranges, originally grafted from a pomegranate tree crossed with an orange, are my favourite. They appear briefly between January and March, and have red-streaked skin and wickedly ruby-red flesh.

The tangerine, mandarin and the satsuma (a seedless variety of the mandarin) make up the basic varieties of loose-skinned citrus. However, years of cross-breeding has produced a succession of what I call 'committee fruit' no doubt dreamed up by marketing departments. Clementine, mineola, ortaline, tangelo, tangor and suntina are examples. There is nothing wrong with these specimens, but do we actually need all of them? I was quite happy with clementines.

Kumquats are like tiny oval oranges with a tart flesh and edible sweet skin. Their fragrant bitter-sweet flavour is a wonderful addition to fruit salads and syrups. They are expensive but a few go a long way.

Choose bright, glossy, unblemished specimens. Loose-skinned citrus should be just that – loose but not squashy. Unfortunately, some oranges and tangerines may taste dry and boring even though they look in good condition. The only safeguard is to buy them from a greengrocer or supermarket known to sell fruit with a good flavour. Store them in the fridge or a cool larder rather than leaving them in the fruit bowl where they will soon start to look unappetizing.

As most of us know, oranges are very high in vitamin C. Unfortunately, only about one quarter is in the flesh and it is easily destroyed by heat or poor storage. They also contain fibre, potassium, calcium and iron. Unusually for fruit, both oranges and clementines are a useful source of B vitamins, especially pyridoxine (B6) and folate.

	Source	Season
Orange	Israel	December–July
	Morocco	December–June
	South Africa	May–November
	Spain	October–July
Clementine	Cyprus	November–March
	France	November–January
	Morocco	November–February
	South Africa	May–September
	Spain	October–May
Satsuma	Argentina	May–September
	South Africa	May–September
	Spain	October–May
	Turkey	November–January
Kumquat	Brazil	July–September
	Israel	November–June
	South Africa	April–August

LEMONS AND LIMES

Lemons and limes are the two fruits I could not live without. They make wonderful desserts, and their zest or juice adds an invigorating lightness and sharpness to pastry, purées, creams and syrups.

As with oranges, look for specimens with a firm, lustrous skin – the thinner-skinned ones usually contain more juice. Keep them in the fridge for up to 2 weeks, and wrap cut fruit in clingfilm.

Lemons and limes contain high levels of vitamin C, as well as useful amounts of potassium, calcium, iron and folate.

	Source	Season
Lemon	Greece	November–March
	Israel	All year
	Italy	All year
	South Africa	May–December
	Spain	All year
Lime	Brazil	All year
	France	May–December
	Mexico	All year

GRAPEFRUIT

The familiar yellow-skinned Jaffa grapefruit has a white flesh with a tangy, refreshing flavour. Sweeter by far is the Sunrise grapefruit from Cyprus with its spectacular deep red flesh. Florida and Texas also produce red-fleshed varieties.

Look for heavy, thin-skinned varieties with a firm round shape. They will store in the fridge for a week or two.

Compared with white-fleshed grapefruit, the pink-fleshed variety are comparatively rich in carotene (vitamin A). Both types contain plenty of vitamin C, potassium, calcium and fibre.

Source	Season
Cyprus	October–May
Israel	October–July
South Africa	May–October
United States	October–June

ORANGE AND DATE SALAD

SERVES 4

A simple and very quickly made dessert, best served chilled.
Being rich in carbohydrate, dates are an effective energy boost.
They are also a good source of potassium, B vitamins and
vitamin C.

7 large oranges
100 g / 4 oz fresh dates, sliced lengthways into slivers
25 g / 1 oz shelled pistachio nuts, finely chopped
2 tbsp clear honey
¼–½ tsp orange-flower water
pinch of ground cinnamon

Squeeze the juice from one of the oranges and set aside. Using
a very sharp knife, cut a horizontal slice from the top and
bottom of the remaining oranges. Remove the remaining peel
and all the white pith by cutting downwards, following the
contours of the fruit.

Cut the flesh horizontally into thin slices, removing any
pips. Arrange the slices on individual serving plates with the
date slivers on top. Sprinkle with the chopped pistachio nuts.

Mix the reserved orange juice with the honey, orange-
flower water and cinnamon. Pour a little over each serving.

GOLDEN CITRUS SALAD

SERVES 6–8

This vibrant salad is stunning to look at. You could use pomegranate seeds, dried cranberries or cherries instead of the redcurrants, and you could try sliced purple figs instead of the plums.

75 g/3 oz caster sugar
5 large oranges
6 clementines
4 dark-skinned plums, cut into thin segments
5 kumquats, thinly sliced
200 g/7 oz lychees, peeled and pitted
75 g/3 oz redcurrants
100 g/4 oz physalis (Cape gooseberries)
3 tbsp grenadine syrup

Put the sugar in a small heavy-based saucepan. Heat gently, stirring constantly, until the sugar melts and becomes caramel-coloured. Be careful not to let it burn. Remove from the heat and pour in 150 ml/¼ pint of cold water. When the spluttering dies down, return the pan to the heat and stir until the caramel dissolves. Leave to cool.

Cut the thinly pared peel from one of the oranges into thin shreds and set the peel aside.

Cut a horizontal slice from the top and bottom of the oranges and tangerines to expose the flesh. Using a very sharp knife, remove the peel and pith by cutting downwards, following the contours of the fruit. Working over a bowl to catch the juice, slice down between the flesh and the membrane of each orange segment, and ease out the flesh. Slice the clementines thinly. Add the juices to the caramel.

Put the oranges and clementines in a large serving bowl with the plums, kumquats, lychees and redcurrants. Set aside 8 physalis as decoration and remove the papery husks from the rest. Add to the fruit in the bowl. Pour over the cold caramel syrup, then cover and chill.

Meanwhile, blanch the reserved orange peel shreds for 3 minutes, then drain. Return to the pan with 150 ml/¼ pint fresh water and the grenadine syrup. Simmer for 12–15 minutes until syrupy and the peel has become deep pink. Remove the shreds from the pan and leave to cool. Scatter the shreds over the salad when ready to serve.

SUNSET JELLY

SERVES 8

I'll never grow out of liking jellies. There is something fascinating about the translucent shimmering colour and the wobbliness. A jelly made with fresh fruit makes a specially welcome dessert after a rich meal. Serve it with crisp vanilla biscuits, such as Langues de Chat. Start the day before you plan to serve the jelly, to allow time for setting. For the most dramatic effect, use grapefruit with really deep pink flesh.

2 large pink-fleshed grapefruit
2 large white-fleshed grapefruit
200 ml/7 fl oz orange juice
juice of ½ lemon
3 tbsp sugar
1 sachet powdered gelatine

Using a very sharp knife, cut a horizontal slice from the top and bottom of the grapefruit. Remove the remaining peel and all the white pith by cutting downwards following the contours of the fruit.

Working over a bowl to catch the juice, cut down between the flesh and the membrane of each segment. Ease out the flesh and put it in a bowl, keeping the two colours separate.

Drain the juice from each bowl and put it all in a measuring jug with the orange and lemon juice. Add sufficient water to make up the liquid to 600 ml/1 pint. Stir in the sugar.

Put 4 tablespoons of the liquid in a small bowl. Sprinkle the gelatine over the surface, then leave for 10 minutes until spongy. Place over a pan of hot water until completely dissolved. Mix with the remaining liquid, stirring thoroughly.

Pour enough liquid to make a 1 cm/½ inch layer into the base of a lightly oiled 1.3 L/2 ¼ pint mould. Chill until set.

Arrange half the pink grapefruit segments in a layer on top of the jelly. Pour over enough liquid to cover. Chill until set. Make another layer with half the white grapefruit segments, cover with more liquid and chill again until set. Repeat the layering and chilling with the remaining segments, finishing with a layer of jelly.

To unmould, dip the mould briefly into hot water. Cover with a plate and invert, then remove the mould.

LEMON POLENTA CAKE

SERVES 8

Served with very cold home-made ice-cream, this makes an excellent dinner-party dessert, and it's just as good as a family tea-time cake too. The cake is light and moist with a pleasantly gritty texture from the polenta – a fine golden cornmeal with a deeply satisfying mild flavour. Instead of butter or margarine, I've used a small amount of olive oil which is high in mono-unsaturated fatty acids.

3 eggs, separated
1½ tbsp olive oil
100 g/4 oz sugar
finely grated zest and juice of 3 lemons
250 g/9 oz ricotta cheese
250 ml/9 fl oz semi-skimmed milk
1 tsp vanilla essence
225 g/8 oz polenta
2 tsp baking powder
50 g/2 oz candied citron or lemon peel, very finely chopped

Lightly grease a 23 cm/9 inch cake tin and dust with flour, shaking out the excess.

Beat together the egg yolks, oil, sugar and lemon zest until the mixture is very thick and pale.

Beat the milk with the ricotta until smooth, then beat this into the egg yolk mixture together with the vanilla essence and the lemon juice.

Next, add the polenta and baking powder, gradually beating them in to avoid lumps forming. Stir in the candied citron, then leave to stand for 15 minutes to soften the polenta.

Whisk the egg whites until stiff, then carefully fold into the polenta mixture using a metal spoon.

Summer Fruit Brioche Pudding *(page 82)*, with berries

Yogurt Ice with Fresh and Dried Cherries *(page 55)*

Melon, Strawberry and Basil Salad *(page 135)*

Mango and Ginger with Passion Fruit Sauce *(page 159)*

Golden Citrus Salad *(page 104)*

Plum Compote with Orange Zest and Rosemary *(page 57)*

Fresh Fig and Raisin Compote *(page 181)*

Pomegranates with Spiced Rice Pudding *(page 190)*

Pour the mixture into the prepared tin. Bake in a preheated oven at 170°C (160°C fan oven)/gas 4 for 50–55 minutes until golden and springy to touch, and a knife inserted in the centre comes out clean.

Leave the cake to cool in the tin for a few minutes, then run a knife round the edge to loosen it. Turn on to a rack and leave to cool completely.

SUSSEX POND PUDDING

SERVES 6

This is a lovely old-fashioned pudding, traditionally made with one whole lemon. I have added a few kumquats and chunks of pink grapefruit and orange for a sweeter flavour. The fruit is cooked with the peel intact, so use unwaxed fruit if possible. Otherwise scrub it well under warm running water, although I'm not sure how effective this is.

100 g/4 oz self-raising flour
100 g/4 oz wholemeal self-raising flour
pinch of salt
100 g/4 oz vegetable suet
150 ml/¼ pint milk or water
1 lemon
1 orange, unpeeled and cut into chunks
½–1 ruby-red grapefruit, unpeeled and cut into chunks
a few kumquats, left whole
75 g/3 oz butter, cut into small chunks
75 g/3 oz sugar

Sift the flours and salt into a bowl, adding the bran from the wholemeal flour. Stir in the suet with a fork. Add the milk and mix to a firm dough. Knead briefly, then roll out thinly to a large circle just under 5 mm/¼ inch thick. Cut out one quarter to use as a lid.

Lightly grease a 1.1 L/2 pint pudding basin. Line it with the pastry, moistening the cut edges and pushing them together to seal. Trim the top neatly, level with the top of the basin. Mix the trimmings with the reserved pastry for the lid.

Put a few chunks of butter in the bottom of the bowl, with 2 tablespoons of sugar. Soften the lemon by rolling it on the work surface, then prick all over with a cocktail stick to allow the juices to flow when cooked. Put the lemon in the middle of the bowl, then fill the cavity round it with the remaining fruit, butter and sugar. It should be tightly packed.

Roll out the remaining pastry to form a lid. Moisten the edges and seal.

Cover with a large piece of foil, pleated down the middle to allow for expansion. Tie securely with string.

Place on a trivet in a deep saucepan, then pour in enough boiling water to come halfway up the sides of the basin. Cover and steam for 2½ hours, topping up the boiling water now and again.

Remove from the pan and allow to settle for 5 minutes. Loosen the edge with the tip of a knife, then invert on to a heated serving dish. Serve immediately with the hot citrusy syrup from the middle of the pudding and a little tender fruit with each portion.

CITRUS SAVARIN WITH FRESH AND DRIED FRUITS

SERVES 10–12

This would make a healthy and lighter alternative to Christmas pudding. Made with citrus juice and honey, the syrup is not nearly so cloying as that which normally oozes from babas and savarins. Try different fillings – pineapple, strawberry and blueberry would be a good combination, or drained fruit from the Khoshaf (page 48).

1 quantity Savarin Dough (page 205)

CITRUS SYRUP
finely grated zest of ½ orange
strained juice of 2 oranges
finely grated zest and juice of 1 lemon
finely grated zest and juice of 1 lime
4 tbsp clear acacia or orange blossom honey
6 tbsp water

FILLING
75 g/3 oz dried pears
50 g/2 oz sugar
450 ml/¾ pint water
1 vanilla pod, split lengthways
1 tsp juniper berries, crushed
600 g/1¼ lb pears
40 g/1½ oz dried cranberries or cherries
15 g/½ oz almonds with skin, sliced lengthways

Lightly grease a 23 cm/9 inch savarin mould. Spoon in the dough and cover with a clean tea towel. Leave to rise in a warm place for about 20 minutes until it almost fills the mould. Bake in a preheated oven at 220°C (210°C fan oven)/gas 7 for 25 minutes.

Meanwhile, make the citrus syrup: put all the ingredients in a saucepan. Cover and simmer over a medium heat for 10 minutes.

Turn the baked savarin out of the mould on to a wire rack set over a large plate. Spoon over the hot syrup while the savarin is still warm. Spoon the syrup which drips on to the plate over the savarin again, until it is all absorbed.

To make the filling, slice the dried pear pieces in half lengthways and put them in a saucepan with the sugar, water, vanilla pod and juniper berries. If you don't like to find whole spices in your dessert, wrap the berries in a piece of muslin so you can fish them out later, but I think they add agreeable bursts of unexpected flavour.

Stir over a medium heat until the sugar has dissolved, then simmer for 10 minutes until the pears are just tender.

Quarter, core and peel the fresh pears. Cut the quarters in half lengthways. Add to the dried pears in the pan and simmer for another 5 minutes until translucent.

Drain, reserving the liquid, and put the pears in a bowl with the cranberries. Remove the vanilla pod, and the juniper berries too, if you don't want to leave them in. Return the liquid to the pan. Boil hard for a few minutes until reduced and syrupy. Pour over the fruit and leave to cool to room temperature, then add the almonds.

Place the savarin on a serving dish and fill the centre with the fruit. Spoon the juices over the savarin.

LIME CREAMS WITH PASSION FRUIT

SERVES 4

The perfumed sweetness of passion fruit is a heavenly combination with the tangy lime cream. Don't be put off by tofu – mixed with eggs and a little sugar, it makes an almost fat-free alternative to cream, and adds protein and calcium. Serve warmish or at room temperature.

almond or grapeseed oil
2 limes
3 eggs
100 g/4 oz firm silken tofu
50 g/2 oz caster sugar
4 passion fruit

Lightly brush four 150 ml/¼ pint ramekins with oil. Have ready a large flat-bottomed steamer basket set over simmering water.

Peel away three thin slivers of lime zest and slice into very thin matchstick strips. Plunge into boiling water for a few minutes, then drain and reserve. Finely grate the remaining zest and squeeze out the juice.

Beat the eggs with the tofu and sugar until very smooth. Stir in the lime zest, together with the strained juice.

Pour the mixture into the prepared ramekins. Cover each one with a greased dome of foil, then place in the steamer basket (cook in batches if your steamer isn't big enough).

Cover and steam for about 8 minutes, or until a knife inserted in the centre comes out clean. Remove from the steamer and leave to stand for 10–15 minutes or until ready to serve.

Run the tip of a knife round the edge and turn out on to individual serving plates. Cut the passion fruit in half, scoop out the pulp and pour it over the creams. Top with the reserved lime zest.

LIME AND PISTACHIO CHEESECAKE

SERVES 8–10

If you're like me and find tofu a bit of a turn-off, try this. Mixed with quark and just a touch of cream cheese, it makes a deliciously smooth low-fat filling, but you'd never guess what was in it.

1 Cheesecake Base (page 200)
250 g / 9 oz firm silken tofu
250 g / 9 oz quark
75 g / 3 oz low-fat cream cheese
100 g / 4 oz sugar
finely grated zest and juice of 3 limes
4 tbsp boiling water
15 g / ½ oz powdered gelatine
15 g / ½ oz shelled pistachio nuts, finely chopped
lime slices, to decorate
slivers of lime zest, to decorate

Lightly grease the base and sides of a 23 cm/9 inch springform tin. Press your chosen base mixture into the tin, and chill or bake according to the recipe.

Beat together the tofu, quark, cream cheese, sugar, and lime zest and juice in a large bowl.

Put the hot water in a small bowl and sprinkle the gelatine over the surface. Leave to dissolve. If necessary, place over a pan of simmering water to get rid of any stubborn lumps.

Pour the gelatine into the tofu mixture, beating well. Pour into the tin and chill for 3–4 hours or overnight.

Carefully remove the cheesecake from the tin. Press the pistachio nuts on to the sides until evenly covered. Decorate the top with thinly sliced pieces of lime and slivers of zest.

LIME HONEYCOMB MOULD

SERVES 6

Usually made with lemons, this is an old-fashioned dessert popular with children. The layer of jelly at the bottom never fails to please.

450 ml / ¾ pint semi-skimmed milk
finely grated zest of 2 limes
juice of 3 limes
3 eggs, separated
75 g / 3 oz sugar
¼ pint single cream
1 sachet powdered gelatine

Pour the milk into a small saucepan, add the lime zest and bring almost to the boil. Remove from the heat and leave to infuse for 15 minutes.

Whisk the egg yolks, sugar, cream and gelatine in a bowl. Gradually whisk in the warm milk. Place over a pan of simmering water and stir for about 5 minutes until the mixture thickens.

Remove from the heat, stir in the lime juice, then strain the mixture into a large bowl.

Whisk the egg whites until stiff, then carefully fold into the custard. Pour into a 1.1 L/2 pint wetted mould, or individual moulds. Chill for 3–4 hours until set.

When ready to serve, run the tip of a knife round the edge and invert on to a plate. If the mould refuses to budge, dip briefly in hot water.

LIME, PISTACHIO AND RICOTTA ICE

SERVES 4–6

Ices made with ricotta cheese are creamy but low in fat, and there's no fussing with egg yolks or making custard. Leave out the pistachios if you wish, but they do add a nice texture and colour. This tastes strongly of limes – best eaten very cold.

finely grated zest of 2 limes
150 ml / ¼ pint strained lime juice (about 5 limes)
150 g / 5 oz caster sugar
350 g / 12 oz ricotta cheese
150 ml / ¼ pint Greek yogurt
40 g / 1½ oz shelled pistachio nuts, roughly chopped
pistachios and lime slices, to decorate

Mix together the lime zest and juice, then add the sugar and stir until dissolved.

Blend the ricotta and yogurt in a food processor until really smooth, then gradually blend in the lime solution.

Freeze in an ice-cream maker, following the manufacturer's instructions, or pour into a shallow freezerproof tray. Cover the surface with clingfilm and freeze until beginning to harden round the edges. Tip into a large bowl and beat until smooth. Repeat the process twice more if you have time, stirring in the pistachios after the final beating. If using an ice-cream maker, add the pistachios towards the end of the churning. Cover and freeze until completely solid.

Put in the fridge for about 30 minutes before serving. Scoop into chilled individual glass serving bowls, and decorate with pistachio nuts and lime slices.

THREE-GRAPEFRUIT SALAD WITH MINT

SERVES 2

Sweet and juicy, ruby and pink grapefruit make a stunning combination with the white-fleshed variety in this refreshing dessert. Serve well chilled. Grapefruit are thought to contain an enzyme which stimulates the metabolism, which perhaps explains why they are often used in slimming diets.

1 ruby-red grapefruit
1 pink-fleshed grapefruit
1 white-fleshed grapefruit
2 tbsp clear honey
finely grated zest of 1 lemon
1 tbsp chopped fresh mint

Using a very sharp knife, cut a horizontal slice from the top and bottom of the grapefruit, exposing the flesh. Remove the remaining peel and all the white pith by cutting downwards, following the contours of the fruit.

Working over a bowl to catch the juice, cut down between the flesh and membrane of each segment. Ease out the flesh and put it in a bowl.

Arrange the segments on individual serving plates, alternating the colours. Chill until ready to serve.

Mix the reserved grapefruit juice with the honey, lemon zest and mint. Pour a little over each serving.

PINK GRAPEFRUIT, PAPAYA AND COCONUT SALAD

SERVES 2–3

This idea came from a recipe leaflet produced by my local greengrocer. The combination of sweetly acidic grapefruit, rich smooth papaya and crunchy coconut is really delicious. The papaya seed garnish adds a lovely peppery taste. You can buy dried coconut ribbons in healthfood shops. Don't be tempted to use desiccated coconut. Papaya is rich in carotene (vitamin A) and vitamin C. Grapefruit is another good source of vitamin C, and is also rich in folate, one of the B vitamins.

2 pink-fleshed grapefruit
1 ripe papaya
juice of ½ lime
sugar, to taste
25 g / 1 oz dried coconut ribbons
papaya seeds, to decorate

Using a very sharp knife, slice the top and bottom off the grapefruit to expose the flesh. Then remove all the remaining peel and white pith by slicing from top to bottom, following the contours of the fruit.

Working over a bowl to catch the juices, cut down between the flesh and the membrane of each segment. Remove the flesh and put in a serving bowl with the juices.

Cut the papayas into quarters and remove the seeds, reserving a teaspoonful for decoration. Cut away the peel, then slice the flesh lengthways into neat segments. Cut each segment in half crossways. Add to the grapefruit in the bowl and sprinkle with the lime juice and sugar to taste. Chill until required.

Remove the fruit from the fridge about 30 minutes before serving. Stir in the coconut ribbons and sprinkle with the reserved papaya seeds. Serve at once while the coconut is still crisp.

BLOOD ORANGE GRANITA

SERVES 6

This flame-coloured crunchy granita is rich but refreshingly tart – perfect after a heavy meal. Serve by itself, or layer in tall glass goblets with Ricotta Cream (page 206) or whipped cream flavoured with finely grated orange zest and a few crushed cardamom seeds. Blood oranges contain five times as much carotene (vitamin A) as ordinary oranges.

12–13 blood oranges
2 tbsp caster sugar, or to taste
2 tbsp orange flavoured liqueur (optional)

Squeeze and strain the juice from the oranges – you'll need 1 L/1¼ pints.

Add the sugar and stir until completely dissolved. Pour the mixture into a shallow freezerproof tray.

When the mixture is almost frozen, mash lightly with a fork so as not to destroy the ice crystals. Stir in the liqueur, if using, and freeze again.

Desserts with
Vine Fruit

Vine fruits include not only grapes but melons, kiwi fruit and passion fruit too. The majority of recipes in this chapter are for refreshing fruit salads and sorbets – the best way to use these luscious and cleansing fruits. Passion fruit is the exception; although irresistible eaten straight from the shell like a boiled egg, they are just as delicious cooked – the heat intensifies their heady fragrance.

GRAPES

Grapes are one of our oldest fruits and have been cultivated for thousands of years. In the past, they were grown mainly for wine, or squeezed for juice, or dried to become currants, sultanas and raisins. Wine grapes are small and sharp-tasting, with tough skins. The widespread use of the larger and sweeter dessert grapes was an early twentieth century development arising from crises in the wine industry and the need to find new markets.

Dessert grapes are generally classified by the colour of their skins: either black or white. To a great extent it is the skins which determine the flavour of the grape. Those with a high tannin content are more astringent. Black grapes have a dusty bloom and range from inky bluish-black to rusty pink. 'White' grapes may be pale green, greenish-gold, or amber. Both types contain seeds, but the seedless varieties are becoming more popular for obvious reasons.

The seedless red Flame grape from the United States is a delicious crisp-textured variety. Plump green seeded Italias have a fragrant musk-scented flavour. Best of all in my opinion are the greenish-gold Muscat grapes, which are enticingly sweet with a strong musky aroma.

Choose plump, unblemished fruit, avoiding those with the slightest hint of browning around the base of the stalk. Grapes should be firmly attached to the stalk, but it is my impression that all but the very best supermarkets have lost sight of this. It's rare nowadays to find carefully displayed grapes nestling safely in tissue paper, and too often I find a bag full of loose grapes once I get them home.

Once cut from the vine, grapes do not ripen further, so buy them in peak condition and eat within a day or two. Store them loosely wrapped in the fridge or a cool larder.

It's with good reason that grapes are the invalid's favourite, or is that a well person's assumption? I think not. When I was newly pregnant and nauseous, grapes were the only food I could face. They are thirst-quenching, easy to digest, and pleasingly small – guaranteed to revive to most fragile of appetites. Grapes have been used for centuries in special diets, detoxifying the body and providing it with water, sugar, fibre, vitamins and minerals. They contain ellagic acid, thought to block the enzymes used by cancer cells. Grapes are rich in carbohydrate too, and make a great energy-giving snack.

Source	Season
Brazil	January–March
Chile	December–June
France	August–October

Israel	May–September
South Africa	December–June
United States	June–January

MELONS

A slice of chilled melon is like nectar on a hot day. When perfectly ripe and intensely flavoured, melons need no other treatment, although you could turn them into a sorbet. Less perfect specimens will benefit from a squeeze of lemon or lime to bring out the flavour.

There's a good choice of melons available all year round, varying greatly in size, colour and flavour. The most widely available is the yellow- or white-skinned Honeydew – somewhat boring, but sweet and cheap. Ogens and Galias, both spherical with greenish-gold skins when ripe, are more expensive but worth buying for their aromatic and succulent green flesh. My favourites are Canteloupe and Charentais. The Canteloupe has a scaly, sometimes grooved skin and orange or green flesh. The Charentais has a pale green stripy skin and orange flesh. Both have a distinctive, intensely perfumed flavour when ripe. Watermelons are enormous with a smooth dark green or mottled light and dark green skin, and bright red flesh. Some varieties are seedless, but I think spitting out the black seeds is part of the pleasure of eating a watermelon.

There's no point in buying a melon unless it's perfectly ripe. It should be heavy for its size, yield when lightly pressed and smell highly perfumed. It's harder to tell with watermelons, which often turn out to be tasteless and woolly instead of sweet and crisp. It's best to buy them cut, or even better, insist on being given a small piece to taste. You probably won't be very popular, but this sensible practice is the norm in countries where watermelons grow.

Most melons store well either at room temperature or in the fridge. Cover melon with clingfilm if you put it in the fridge, otherwise the smell will permeate other foods.

All melons contain useful amounts of vitamin C, potassium and fibre. Being 95 per cent water, they are low in calories. Together with mangoes and physalis, orange-fleshed Canteloupe melons contain enormously high levels of carotene (vitamin A), more than any other fruit.

Source	Season
Brazil	October–May
France	June–October
Holland	May–October
Israel	March–December
Spain	March–October
Italy	July–September

KIWI FRUIT

Originally known as the Chinese Gooseberry after its country of origin, this ubiquitous fruit was renamed to reflect the fact that New Zealand is the main producer and responsible for its commercial success. However, most kiwi fruit sold in Britain now come from Italy.

During the 1980s, kiwi fruit suffered from over-exposure, popping up without fail on artfully arranged plates of designer food. They are now considered a bit of a culinary cliché by some, but I like to use them now and again. They're versatile, cheap and packed with nutrients.

Beneath the fuzzy brown skin lies brilliant green juicy flesh, spectacularly studded with black seeds radiating from a creamy core. The flavour is both acidic and sweet.

Kiwi fruit are ready to eat when the flesh yields to gentle pressure. Firm specimens will ripen at room temperature, especially if placed near apples and bananas. Ripe kiwi fruit can be stored in the fridge for several days.

Kiwi fruit contain an enormous amount of vitamin C, weight for weight as much as an orange. They are rich in potassium and are a useful source of calcium, magnesium and iron. They contain a small amount of pyridoxine (vitamin B6).

Source	Season
Israel	October–March
Italy	November–May
New Zealand	April–January
United States	October–February

PASSION FRUIT

Don't be put off by passion fruit's unprepossessing exterior. Beneath the wrinkled grey-brown shell lies the gateway to paradise. Words cannot describe the seductive intense fragrance of the pulp inside. It is quinces, guavas, pears, limes and strawberries all rolled into one. The pulp itself is a startlingly vivid mix of luminous yellow-green jelly dotted with black tear-drop seeds. The seeds are edible and are part of the pleasure of the fruit, although you can sieve them out if you prefer to.

Slice off the top and eat the pulp raw, in polite circles with a teaspoon, or slurping it straight from the shell when you're on your own. The pulp makes a marvellous sorbet and a wonderfully refreshing sauce for all manner of desserts. It also adds zest and sparkle to mousses and soufflés.

Choose the largest fruits you can find, avoiding those with cracked skins. A wrinkled skin is supposed to be a sign of ripeness, but it's also a sign of age. I don't think the state of the skin makes a lot of difference to the flavour.

Because of their stout skins, passion fruit survive transportation remarkably well, and they can be stored in the fridge for up to 2 weeks without loss of quality.

Passion fruit are a great ingredient in healthy fruit desserts. They contain good amounts of fibre, potassium, magnesium, iron, zinc and carotene (vitamin A), as well as small but useful amounts of riboflavin (vitamin B2) and niacin (vitamin B3), which we need for the release of energy from food.

Source	Season
Brazil	January–July
Kenya	All year
New Zealand	February–April

BLACK GRAPES AND LYCHEES WITH ALMOND JELLY AND LIME SYRUP

SERVES 4

A simple but dramatic fruit salad of contrasting colours and flavours. The almonds need plenty of time for soaking, so make the jelly the day before you plan to serve it. I have used ratafia rather than almond essence because I find it is less bitter. Agar–agar, a dried seaweed, is a vegetarian alternative to gelatine. Although used only in small quantities, it is extremely rich in fibre, calcium, iron and zinc. Lychees are a useful source of vitamin C.

225 g/8 oz large black grapes
275 g/10 oz fresh lychees
shelled pistachio nuts, chopped, to decorate

ALMOND JELLY
225 g/8 oz ground almonds
2 tbsp agar–agar
50 g/2 oz sugar
a few drops of ratafia essence
almond or grapeseed oil, for greasing

LIME SYRUP
200 ml/7 fl oz water
50 g/2 oz sugar
finely grated zest of ½ lime

To make the almond jelly, soak the almonds in 300 ml/½ pint of cold water for at least 4 hours or overnight. Strain through a muslin-lined sieve, twisting the muslin tightly round the almonds to squeeze out as much liquid as possible. You should end up with about 150 ml/¼ pint.

Put 300 ml/½ pint of water and the agar-agar in a saucepan. Bring to the boil, then simmer until the agar-agar has dissolved completely. Stir in the sugar, the almond liquid and a few drops of ratafia. Pour into a lightly greased 18 cm/7 inch square tin. Allow to cool, then put in the fridge to set.

To make the lime syrup, put the water, sugar and lime zest in a small saucepan. Heat gently until the sugar has dissolved, then boil for 2 minutes until syrupy. Leave to cool.

Meanwhile, halve the grapes, removing the seeds, and put the grapes in a serving bowl.

Peel the lychees over a bowl, reserving the juice. Cut the flesh vertically into quarters and remove the stone. Add the flesh and juice to the grapes. Cover and chill.

To serve, slice the jelly diagonally into small diamond shapes. Place 4–6 diamonds on individual serving plates. Arrange the lychees and grapes attractively on top. Spoon over a little lime syrup and sprinkle with chopped pistachio nuts.

GRAPE, KIWI FRUIT AND ORANGE TERRINE

SERVES 8

This is a very clean-tasting jelly with no added sugar. It's delicious served with Mixed Berry Sauce (page 218). Be sure to allow each layer to set before adding the next. If the juice sets too much while you are waiting for the layers to chill, place it over a pan of simmering water, then allow to cool.

500 ml/18 fl oz freshly squeezed orange juice
(about 5 large oranges)
2 tbsp powdered gelatine
450 ml/¾ pint clear apple juice
2 kiwi fruit, thinly sliced
350 g/12 oz large black grapes, halved and deseeded
frosted grapes and mint leaves (page 218), to decorate

Put a 1.5 L/2½ pint terrine dish in the freezer to chill.

Put 6 tablespoons of the orange juice in a bowl. Sprinkle the gelatine over the surface and leave for 10 minutes until spongy. Place over a pan of hot water until completely dissolved.

Add to the remaining orange juice, mixing well. Add the apple juice and mix well again. Pour through a muslin-lined sieve into a jug.

Pour a 1 cm/½ inch layer of juice over the base of the chilled dish and chill until set.

Arrange a layer of kiwi fruit on top of the jelly and pour over enough juice to cover. Chill until set. Next, arrange a layer of grapes over the jelly, cover with more juice and chill again until set. Repeat the layering and chilling until all the grapes and kiwi fruit have been used up, ending with a deep layer of jelly. Chill overnight until set.

To serve, dip the base of the terrine in hot water for a few seconds, or cover with a tea towel wrung out in hot water. Carefully turn out on to a serving plate. Decorate with frosted grapes and mint leaves. Slice carefully using a very sharp knife.

GRAPE FLAN WITH RICOTTA CREAM

SERVES 4–6

You might think this is a calorie-packed dessert but the sponge base contains hardly any fat, and ricotta cream has about one quarter the fat of double cream. Grapes contain a fair amount of carbohydrate, and are therefore an effective energy boost.

½ quantity Ricotta Cream (page 206)
1 × 23 cm/9 inch Fatless Whisked Sponge Base (page 198)
100 g/4 oz each red and green seedless grapes, halved

Using a palette knife, spread the ricotta cream over the flan base.

Arrange the grapes cut-side down on top of the cream in alternate circles of red and green, overlapping them slightly so that the base is well filled.

MELON COCKTAIL WITH GINGER, CHILLI AND MINT SYRUP

SERVES 6

Ginger, chilli and mint are all known to aid digestion, so this is good to serve after a rich meal. The syrup is mellow-flavoured with just the slightest hint of heat from the chilli. The mint cuts the sweetness. Allow plenty of time for chilling.

1 large Charentais or Canteloupe melon (about 1.6 kg/3½ lb)
225 g/8 oz black grapes
175 g/6 oz cherries
fresh mint sprigs, to decorate

SYRUP
200 g/7 oz sugar
300 ml/½ pint water
2 thinly pared strips orange peel
finely grated zest of 1 lime
2–3 thin slices stem ginger
2 tsp syrup from the ginger jar
½ fresh green chilli, deseeded
4 fresh mint sprigs

First make the syrup: put the sugar and water in a small saucepan with the rest of the ingredients. Stir over a low heat until the sugar has dissolved, then boil for 5–7 minutes until syrupy. Leave to cool, then strain.

Halve the melon, scoop out the seeds and remove the flesh with a melon baller. To make perfect melon balls, press the baller deep into the flesh, concave side down, until the juice comes through the hole in the bottom of the baller. Twist to remove the ball. Either eat the leftover melon flesh or use it in a sorbet. Put the melon balls in a serving bowl.

Halve the grapes, removing the seeds if necessary, and add to the melon. Add the cherries, leaving them whole if you don't mind the stones, otherwise remove them with a stoner, trying not to destroy their shape too much.

Pour the syrup over the fruit, cover and chill. Decorate with mint sprigs just before serving.

GRAPES WITH ORANGE AND STAR ANISE

SERVES 2–3

A perfect bunch of grapes with the bloom intact makes a convenient dessert for unexpected guests when you're short of time. But if your bunch of grapes sports bare stalks or you simply have a lot of loose grapes, try this.

350 g / 12 oz grapes, preferably a mixture of black, green and red
75 g / 3 oz sugar
200 ml / 7 fl oz water
3 thinly pared strips of orange peel, cut into needle shreds
crushed seeds from 2 star anise pods

Halve the grapes, removing the seeds if necessary. Divide the grapes among individual serving bowls and put in the fridge to chill.

Put the sugar and water in a small saucepan with the orange peel shreds and crushed star anise seeds. Stir over a medium heat until the sugar has dissolved, then boil hard for 5 minutes until syrupy. Allow to cool a little, then pour over the grapes, making sure each serving gets a few orange shreds.

Leave the grapes to macerate in the fridge for as long as possible before serving.

MELON, STRAWBERRY AND BASIL SALAD

SERVES 6

Use a perfectly ripe melon and strawberries with a good flavour – inferior or unripe fruit will not stand up to the assertive flavour of the basil. Shred the basil with your fingers rather than chopping it, otherwise it will bruise. Canteloupe melons contain about twenty times more carotene (vitamin A) than green-fleshed Honeydew melons.

1 large Canteloupe melon
350 g / 12 oz strawberries
juice of 1 orange
3–4 large fresh basil leaves, torn into shreds
100 g / 4 oz raspberries
tiny fresh basil sprigs, to decorate
caster sugar, to taste

Cut the melon in half and remove the seeds. Cut the flesh into balls with a melon baller and put in a serving bowl.

Slice the strawberries in half, or into quarters if they are very large, and add to the melon balls. Stir in the orange juice and the basil.

Leave to stand at room temperature for an hour to allow the flavours to mingle.

Just before serving, scatter the raspberries over the top. Add the basil sprigs and sprinkle with caster sugar to taste.

FOUR MELON SALAD WITH PASSION FRUIT AND CHILLI SALSA

SERVES 4–6

Don't be alarmed by the chilli – the flavour is very mild. The idea comes from the Mexican tradition of eating thirst-quenching slices of orange sprinkled with dried chilli flakes. The heat of the chillies makes you sweat, which is nature's way of cooling the body. Use a very sharp knife to dice the fruit for the salsa, otherwise it will turn into a mush instead of nice distinct shapes. The salsa should be eaten within 3–4 hours as it does not keep well.

½ Honeydew melon
½ Galia melon
1 small Charentais melon
450 g / 1 lb watermelon

SALSA
3 passion fruit
1 blood orange
2 kiwi fruit, finely diced
4 tbsp finely diced mango flesh
1–2 small green chillies, deseeded and very finely diced
1½ tbsp fresh lime juice

To make the salsa, scoop out the passion fruit pulp and put in a small bowl.

Next, cut a slice from the top and bottom of the orange. Remove the skin and all the white pith by cutting from top to bottom, following the contours of the orange. Working over a bowl to catch the juice, cut down between the flesh and membrane of each segment and remove the segments. Slice the flesh crossways into very small pieces and add to the passion fruit in the bowl, together with the juice.

Mix in the kiwi fruit, mango flesh, chillies and lime juice. Put in the fridge while you prepare the melons.

Cut the melons lengthways into neat segments. Scoop out the pips and remove the skin. Arrange one or two segments of each type on individual serving plates. Spoon the salsa down the middle of the segments and serve at once.

THREE-MELON SORBET

SERVES 8

This very pretty dessert is wonderfully refreshing on a hot evening. Freezing makes flavours less intense, so make sure all your melons are perfectly ripe and taste strongly of melon. You will need roughly equal amounts of each type. Eat within a day or two of making, before the flavour starts to escape. Exotic fruit juice concentrate is sold in good healthfood shops. It is naturally sweet and adds to the flavour. Melons are a useful source of vitamin C, and the orange-fleshed varieties contain amazingly high levels of carotene (vitamin A).

700 g / 1½ lb wedge of watermelon, preferably the seedless variety
juice of 2 limes
75 ml / 3 fl oz exotic fruit juice concentrate
1 large ripe green-fleshed melon, such as Ogen or Galia
1 large ripe orange-fleshed melon, such as Charentais or Canteloupe

Cut two thin lengthways slices from the watermelon with the skin still attached. Cover and reserve in the fridge.

Combine the lime juice and exotic fruit juice concentrate, mixing well.

Remove the seeds from the remaining watermelon, if necessary, and cut off the skin. Halve the other two melons and scoop out the seeds. Cut into segments and remove the skin.

Keeping the different colours separate, chop the flesh of all three melons into cubes. Still keeping each type separate, put in a blender with one-third of the exotic fruit juice solution, and purée until very smooth.

Freeze in an ice-cream maker, following the manufacturer's instructions, or pour into three shallow freezerproof trays. Cover the surface with clingfilm and freeze until beginning to harden around the edges. Tip into a mixing bowl and beat until smooth, then cover and freeze again. Repeat the process twice more if you have time, then freeze until completely hard.

Put in the fridge to soften about 30 minutes before serving. Chill individual tall serving glasses. Cut the reserved watermelon into triangles with the skin still attached.

When ready to serve, spoon scoops of each colour into the glasses and decorate with a watermelon wedge.

MELON, GRAPE AND BLUEBERRY SALAD

SERVES 4

A quickly made but impressive dessert of rich colours. You can use raspberries instead of blueberries. If Charentais melon is unavailable, use another orange-fleshed type such as Cantaloupe. Both types are packed with carotene (vitamin A).

1 large Charentais melon weighing about 1.1 kg/2½ lb
Raspberry/Mixed Berry Sauce (page 218)
225 g/8 oz seedless red grapes
100 g/4 oz blueberries
tiny fresh mint sprigs, to decorate

Cut the melon in half and remove the seeds. Using a melon-baller, cut the flesh into neat balls.

Spoon some of the sauce on to individual serving plates. Arrange the melon balls, grapes and blueberries on top. Decorate with mint sprigs and serve at once.

KIWI FRUIT AND STRAWBERRY ROULADE

SERVES 6–8

Some people consider kiwi fruit to be rather dated, but I still like to use them occasionally. They're relatively cheap, convenient to use, store well and are packed with vitamin C.

1 Fatless Whisked Sponge mixture (page 198), using 3 eggs

FILLING
200 g / 7 oz ricotta cheese
3 tbsp yogurt
finely grated zest of ½ orange
1 tbsp sugar
3 kiwi fruit
150 g / 5 oz strawberries

Lightly oil and line a 33 × 23 cm/13 × 9 inch Swiss roll tin with baking parchment. Sprinkle with flour and knock off any excess.

Pour the whisked sponge mixture into the prepared tin, levelling and pushing the mixture into the corners with a palette knife. Bake in a preheated oven at 220°C (210°C fan oven)/gas 7 for 8–9 minutes until golden and springy to touch.

Turn out on to a sheet of lightly sugared greaseproof paper. Peel off the baking parchment, then roll up from the narrow end, with the greaseproof paper inside. Allow to cool.

Mix together the ricotta, yogurt, orange zest and sugar. Unroll the cooked base and remove the greaseproof paper. Spread the ricotta mixture over the surface, leaving a 1 cm/ ½ inch margin all round.

Peel the kiwi fruit. Slice one of them in half lengthways. Cut one of the halves lengthways into thin segments and reserve as decoration, together with one sliced strawberry. Chop the rest of the kiwi fruit and strawberries and scatter over the ricotta.

Roll up again and place on a serving dish, seam side down. Decorate with kiwi segments and strawberry slices.

KIWI FRUIT AND BANANA SLUSH

SERVES 2

A quickly made dessert for a boost of energy and vitamins. Eat as it is or freeze for a delicious sorbet. It's not absolutely necessary to sieve out the seeds. They add extra fibre but they do turn the purée into an unappetizing shade of khaki.

8 kiwi fruit
1 banana
juice of 2 limes
1 tbsp sugar, or to taste
2 tbsp wholemilk organic yogurt
2 strawberries, to decorate

Peel the kiwi fruit, chop the flesh roughly and purée in a blender until smooth. Push through a fine sieve to get rid of the seeds, then return the purée to the blender.

Slice the banana and add to the purée with the lime juice and sugar. Purée again.

Pour the mixture into individual serving glasses, then chill. When ready to serve, swirl in the yogurt and top with a strawberry.

GREEN AND RED FRUITS WITH LIME CREAM

SERVES 4

Brilliant red pomegranate seeds contrast beautifully with the green fruit. Don't add the seeds until the last minute or they will turn the juice brown. If pomegranates are out of season, use redcurrants or tiny wild strawberries instead.

½ Galia melon
2 kiwi fruit
175 g/6 oz seedless green grapes, halved
2 tbsp caster sugar, or to taste
finely grated zest and juice of 3 limes
1 quantity Ricotta Cream (page 206)
1 pomegranate

Scoop out the melon flesh with a baller and put in a bowl. You will need about 150 g/5 oz.

Peel the kiwi fruit and slice crossways, then cut into segments. Add to the melon in the bowl. Mix in the grapes, sugar and two-thirds of the lime juice. Cover and chill for an hour or two.

Mix the remaining lime juice and two-thirds of the zest with the ricotta cream.

When ready to serve, cut open the pomegranate and extract the seeds. Add to the chilled fruit, reserving a few seeds for decoration.

Divide the fruit among individual glass serving bowls. Spoon or pipe the lime cream over the top, then decorate with the reserved pomegranate seeds and a sprinkling of lime zest. Serve at once.

PASSION FRUIT PUDDING

SERVES 4

A variation on the classic lemon 'surprise' pudding, in which a light sponge topping reveals a creamy layer of fragrant passion fruit. Serve hot or warm – the pudding will sink as it cools.

10 passion fruit
juice of 1 lime
25 g / 1 oz self-raising flour
25 g / 1 oz wholemeal self-raising flour
50 g / 2 oz butter or sunflower margarine
finely grated zest of 2 limes
75 g / 3 oz caster sugar
2 eggs, separated
300 ml / ½ pint semi-skimmed milk

Cut the passion fruit in half and scoop out the pulp. Push through a sieve to get rid of the seeds. Put the juice in a measuring jug with the strained lime juice – you will need 100–125 ml / 3½–4 fl oz.

Sift the flours, returning to the bowl the bran from the wholemeal flour.

Cream the butter or margarine with the lime zest and sugar until light and fluffy. Next, beat in the egg yolks, followed by the flours. Mix in the milk, then the passion fruit and lime juice.

Whisk the egg whites until stiff but not dry, then carefully fold them into the passion fruit mixture.

Pour into a lightly greased 1.1 L / 2 pint ovenproof bowl. Set it in a roasting tin of cold water. Bake in a preheated oven at 180°C (170°C fan oven)/gas 4, for 45 minutes until golden brown and springy to touch.

HOT PASSION FRUIT SOUFFLÉS

SERVES 8

Wonderfully light and airy, these soufflés are like fragrant clouds. They will sink as they cool, so serve them quickly. Make a slit in the top and pour in a little of the sauce. If you do not have eight ramekins, use one large dish.

almond or grapeseed oil
14–15 passion fruit
3 egg yolks
75 g/3 oz sugar
5 egg whites
strained juice of 2 limes

Lightly oil eight 150 ml/¼ pint ramekins.

Halve the passion fruit and scoop out the pulp. Push through a sieve, discarding all but 1 tablespoon of the seeds. You will need 150 ml/¼ pint strained juice.

Beat the egg yolks with all but 2 tablespoons of the sugar for about 3 minutes until pale and thick. Beat in 100 ml/3½ fl oz of the passion fruit pulp.

Whisk the egg whites until soft peaks form, then gradually beat in 1 tablespoon of the sugar until smooth and satiny.

Carefully fold one-third of the egg whites into the passion fruit mixture to slacken it, then gently fold in the rest.

Pour into the prepared ramekins. Bake in a preheated oven at 180°C (170°C fan oven)/gas 4 for 20–30 minutes, until well risen. Meanwhile, put the remaining passion fruit juice in a small saucepan with the lime juice, reserved passion fruit seeds and the last of the sugar. Heat gently, then pour into a small jug and serve with the soufflés.

Desserts with Tropical Fruit

Supermarkets abound with tropical exotica which all too often do not live up to expectations. The flavour, aroma and texture are usually a million miles from that of fruit picked, transported and eaten at the point of perfect ripeness. For that you have to be willing to pay their air fares. I've therefore restricted the fruits in this chapter to those which stand a chance of tasting as they should.

BANANAS

Bananas are one of the most ancient and widely cultivated fruits in the world. Interestingly, they are the flowers of a giant herb, but unlike most flowers, they are sterile and incapable of pollination. It was for this reason that Buddha made the banana plant the symbol of the futility of earthly possessions.

Bananas top the popularity charts in Britain – hardly surprising, since they are the ultimate convenience food, requiring neither washing, peeling nor preparation. That said, a grilled or baked banana is worth the minimal effort required. The sweet creamy flesh becomes bubbling nectar, especially with a slug of rum or orange-flavoured liqueur.

Bananas are normally picked and shipped green. They are stored in special banana-ripening rooms and sold at varying stages of ripeness. The riper the flesh, the sweeter the flavour. Buy your bananas slightly green if you're not going to eat them right away. They will continue to ripen in the fruit bowl. Otherwise look for firm, evenly yellow ones. Don't store bananas in the fridge or they will turn black.

Bananas contain very high levels of potassium – one will provide nearly a fifth of the recommended daily intake. Easily digestible, they provide energy in a concentrated slow-release form, making them a popular snack with athletes and long-distance cyclists. They contain more magnesium than most other fruit, as well as useful levels of vitamins C and B6.

Source	Season
Caribbean	All year
Central America	All year
Colombia	All year
Ivory Coast	All year

MANGOES

Mangoes are one of the most delicious tropical fruits, fortunately becoming more commonplace and usually of good quality. There are an unbelievable number of varieties – probably over 2,500 – although very few find their way to Britain. The large Haden from the Gambia is a good, not too fibrous variety; smaller Alphonsos are also popular, as are Tommy Atkins from Puerto Rico.

Mangoes come in a rainbow-like range of colours – green, yellow, orange, red, maroon – and in many shapes and sizes. The smallest are about the size of a peach, and the largest may be as big as a medium-sized melon. The flesh is deep orange, sometimes slightly fibrous and simply dripping with juice. It's delicious served raw in wedges, sprinkled with lime juice, or puréed.

The colour of the skin is no indication of ripeness. You need to lightly press the flesh, which, as a friend once remarked, should feel like a firm breast. Mangoes continue to ripen slowly even when picked while still hard. A few days, or even weeks, in a warm room can work wonders with hard fruit.

Mangoes contain more carotene (vitamin A) than any other fruit, weight for weight over four times more than an apricot. They also contain vitamins C and E which, together with carotene, are powerful anti-oxidants known to help prevent some cancers. They contain plenty of fibre and small amounts of B vitamins.

Source	Season
Brazil	October–March
Gambia	July–August
Mexico	March–October
Philippines	June–August
Puerto Rico	April–June

PAPAYAS

This large pear-shaped fruit has a green skin streaked with yellow, turning almost completely yellow when ripe. It has luscious pink flesh with a creamy texture and refreshing flavour. It is eaten raw and mixes beautifully with more acidic fruit such as pineapple or pink grapefruit. The central cavity is filled with black edible seeds which add an interesting crunch and a peppery flavour to the raw papaya flesh. They look good too, sprinkled over ices and fruit salads, but use less rather than more, as they can have a dramatic laxative effect.

Choose unblemished firm fruit which gives when lightly pressed. As long as there is a ring of yellow around the stalk end, a green papaya will ripen at room temperature. Without the yellow ring it will never ripen. Once fully ripened, papayas do not last long and should be eaten immediately or stored in the fridge for no more than a day or two.

Papayas contain enzymes which break down protein and are thought to aid digestion, so they're good to serve after a heavy meal. The seeds are used to tenderize meat. Like most orange-fleshed fruits and vegetables, papayas are rich in carotene (vitamin A). They contain plenty of vitamin C, and small but useful amounts of fibre, calcium and magnesium.

Source	Season
Brazil	All year
Canary Islands	January–February
Israel	May–August
South Africa	July–August

PINEAPPLES

Although they've been eaten in Britain for several hundred years, and are available all year round, pineapples still convey a sense of the exotic. A perfectly ripe pineapple is a complex mixture of sweetness and acidity, and needs nothing more than a splash of kirsch or rum. Pineapple is also very good grilled – the high sugar content makes it blacken nicely at the edges – and served with a scoop of very cold ice-cream.

Choose pineapple with a good colour, lively grey–green leaves with a nice bloom, and no bruising. If the pineapple is in prime condition, you should be able to gently pull a leaf from the centre. Smell the base of the fruit – the aroma should shout of pineapple if it is fresh and ripe. If it doesn't, it never will, and means the fruit has been picked unripe. A pineapple will keep for two or three days in the fridge, but allow to come to room temperature before using, to bring out the flavour.

Pineapples are a useful source of vitamin C, fibre, calcium and magnesium. Like the papaya, they contain an enzyme which breaks down protein, so they're good to serve after a heavy meat meal. This also explains why gelatine, which contains animal protein, will not set when used with uncooked pineapple: cooking destroys the enzyme.

Source	Season
Brazil	All year
Ivory Coast	All year
Puerto Rico	All year
South Africa	All year

GUAVAS

The guava is a highly aromatic fruit, the smell of which you will either love or hate. The fruit is pear-shaped, slightly larger than an egg, with a soft delicate skin which may be rough or smooth, green, yellow or wine-red, depending on variety. The flesh ranges from white to yellow to pink. They can be eaten raw, scooping the flesh out of the skin like an avocado, or puréed or lightly stewed, perhaps in a lime-scented syrup. The deeply fragrant flesh makes marvellous ice-cream.

Choose firm fruit which gives when lightly pressed. The skin should be free from dark patches. Handle with care as they are easily damaged. Eat ripe guavas right away, or store in the fridge for no more than a day or two, well covered and away from other foods.

Guavas contain an astonishing amount of vitamin C, weight for weight over four times as much as an orange. They're also a good source of carotene (vitamin A), fibre and potassium.

Source	Season
Brazil	All year
Thailand	All year
Venezuela	August–September

BAKED BANANAS WITH CLEMENTINE AND CARDAMOM CREAM

SERVES 4

Clementines and cardamom add a touch of zest to the soft sweetness of the bananas. If you're lucky enough to have any quince jelly, you could use that instead of marmalade – the combination with bananas is quite heavenly. Bananas are rich in potassium and energy-giving carbohydrate, while clementines are a good source of vitamin C and folate, one of the B vitamins, needed especially towards the end of pregnancy.

3 clementines
2 tbsp marmalade, sieved
1 tbsp lemon juice
4 slightly under-ripe bananas
seeds from 8 cardamom pods, crushed
1 quantity Low-Fat Thick Cream (page 207) or
8 tbsp whipping cream, whipped

Using a swivel peeler, carefully peel the skin from two of the clementines, taking care not to include the bitter pith. Cut the peel into very fine matchstick threads. Plunge the threads into boiling water for 1–2 minutes, then drain and set aside.

Squeeze the juice from all the clementines, straining out any pips.

Melt the marmalade in a small saucepan. Remove from the heat and mix with the lemon juice and all but 3 tablespoons of the clementine juice.

Peel the bananas and slice in half lengthways. Place in a shallow baking dish. Spoon over the marmalade mixture and sprinkle with half the cardamom seeds. Bake in a preheated oven at 220°C (210°C fan oven)/gas 7 for 20–25 minutes until soft.

Stir the remaining clementine juice into the cream.

Arrange the bananas on individual serving plates and pour over the juices. Top with the cream and sprinkle with the remaining cardamom seeds. Decorate with the clementine peel threads and serve at once.

BANANA AND LEMON BALOUZA

SERVES 4–5

A balouza is a traditional Middle Eastern dessert – a beautiful opalescent jelly which looks like moonstones, and wobbles like a belly-dancer's tummy. This version was made for me in Israel by the grandmother of an Iraqi friend.

75 g/3 oz cornflour
1.1 L/2 pints water
150 g/5 oz sugar
3 tbsp lemon juice
3 bananas
25 g/1 oz shelled pistachio nuts
medium or heavy Sugar Syrup (page 210),
made with finely grated lemon zest, or
Lavender Syrup (page 216)

Mix the cornflour to a thin smooth paste with a little of the water. Pour into a saucepan with the rest of the water and the sugar. Stir vigorously with a wooden spoon until the sugar has dissolved.

Slowly bring to the boil, stirring constantly – this will take about 5 minutes. Stir over a very low heat for another 8–10 minutes, until the mixture thickens. It is ready when a teaspoonful solidifies when dropped on a cold plate.

Stir in the lemon juice and cook for a few more minutes, continuing to stir.

Remove from the heat and allow to cool a little. Slice the bananas thinly and stir into the jelly, making sure they are evenly distributed. Pour into individual glass dishes and chill until set.

Cover the pistachios with boiling water. Leave to stand for 5 minutes, then slip off their skins and chop roughly.

Spoon over a little lemon or lavender syrup before serving, then sprinkle with the pistachios.

BANANAS WITH RICOTTA CREAM AND STRAWBERRY SAUCE

SERVES 3

This is a sort of grown-up nursery dessert – the strawberry sauce makes terrific swirls in the cream. If you don't have coconut ribbons, use toasted flaked almonds instead. Serve well chilled. This is an excellent source of vitamin C and potassium, and, considering the creaminess, surprisingly low in fat.

3 ripe bananas
1 quantity Ricotta Cream (page 206)
15 g/ g/½ oz coconut ribbons
100 g/4 oz strawberries
1 tsp sugar
1 tsp lemon juice

Cut the bananas into thin diagonal slices and divide among three individual serving bowls. Pour over enough ricotta cream to cover the bananas. Cover and put in the fridge to chill.

Spread out the coconut ribbons on a baking sheet, and toast in a moderate oven for 2–3 minutes until golden.

Purée the strawberries in a blender with the sugar and lemon juice. Push through a sieve if you want a very smooth sauce. Spoon over the bananas and sprinkle with the coconut.

MANGO AND LIME RICE PUDDING

SERVES 6

A rice pudding with vibrant flavours, inspired by a recipe in Dharamjit Singh's classic *Indian Cookery*. I use the slightly aromatic long-grained Thai fragrant (jasmine) rice. Its slightly sticky texture is perfect for puddings. Mangoes are very rich in carotene (vitamin A) and contain a reasonable amount of vitamin C.

200 g/7 oz Thai fragrant rice
50 g/2 oz sugar
2 ripe mangoes, weighing about 225 g/8 oz each
150 ml/¼ pint whipping cream or Greek yogurt
finely grated zest and juice of 1 lime
butter

Put the rice in a saucepan and cover with water to a depth of 2.5 cm/1 inch. Bring to the boil, then cover tightly and simmer over a very low heat until the water has been absorbed and the rice is very soft. Stir in half the sugar.

Meanwhile, peel the mango and roughly chop the flesh. Put in a blender and purée until smooth. Stir in the cream or yogurt, lime zest, juice and remaining sugar.

Lightly grease a deep 1.1 L/2 pint ovenproof dish. Spoon a layer of rice over the bottom, followed by a layer of mango purée. Repeat the layering, finishing with a layer of mango purée.

Dot with butter and bake in a preheated oven at 150°C (130°C fan oven)/gas 2 for 45–60 minutes until golden round the edges. Serve hot or cold.

MANGO AND BLOOD ORANGE MOUSSE

SERVES 4

This super-healthy dessert is bursting with carotene (vitamin A) and vitamin C. For maximum flavour, make sure you use a really ripe mango. If blood oranges are out of season use two large ordinary oranges instead. This contains uncooked egg white, so keep well chilled and consume within 24 hours.

3 blood oranges
1 mango, weighing about 225 g/8 oz
2 tbsp sugar
2 tsp powdered gelatine
1 egg white
4 passion fruit
toasted coconut ribbons, to decorate

Using a small sharp knife, remove the peel and all the pith from the oranges. Working over a sieve placed over a bowl, remove the flesh by slicing between each segment and the membrane. Reserve the flesh and juice; discard the membrane and pips.

Peel the mango, remove the stone and roughly chop the flesh. Put in a blender with the orange flesh and sugar, and purée until smooth. Transfer to a bowl.

Put the orange juice in a small bowl and sprinkle the gelatine over the surface. Leave for 10 minutes until spongy, then place over a pan of hot water until fully dissolved. Stir into the purée, mixing well.

Whisk the egg white until stiff. Using a metal spoon, fold about one-third of the egg white into the purée to slacken it, then carefully fold in the rest. Put the mixture in a large serving bowl or individual bowls, and chill for 2 hours until set.

Halve the passion fruit and scoop out the pulp. Sieve if you don't like the seeds, but ideally leave them in. Spoon a layer of pulp over the mousse and decorate with toasted coconut ribbons.

MANGO WITH CITRUS SALSA

SERVES 4

In Mexico, street vendors sell slices of mango sprinkled with a mouth-puckering salsa of chilli powder, salt and lime juice. This is a less fiery version which you'll find surprisingly refreshing on a hot day. Best eaten with your hands, either in the bath or a swimming pool.

juice of 2 oranges
juice of 2 limes
pinch of sea salt
pinch of cayenne
dash of Tabasco sauce
4 large ripe mangoes
lime wedges
small triangles of watermelon with skin attached

Combine the orange and lime juice, and season to taste with salt, cayenne and Tabasco. If you want to check the seasoning, try it with a small piece of mango – it tastes quite different on its own.

With the narrow side facing you, slice the mangoes vertically down one side about 2.5 cm/1 inch away from the centre – you should just miss the stone. Repeat with the other side. Use the flesh attached to the stone in another dish, or eat it yourself.

Using the tip of a very sharp knife, cut through the flesh in a diagonal lattice, down to, but not through, the skin. Repeat with the remaining halves.

With the cut side upwards, press the skin inwards so that the flesh opens out into cubes. Arrange on a large serving dish and spoon the citrus juices over the top. Scatter over a few lime wedges and small triangles of watermelon. Serve at once.

MANGO AND GINGER WITH PASSION FRUIT SAUCE

SERVES 6

A zinging dessert full of seductive flavours and textures – little bursts of ginger, luscious mango purée and fragrant passion fruit with crunchy seeds. Make sure your mangoes are perfectly ripe.

2–3 mangoes, about 1.4 kg/3 lb total weight
2.5 cm/1 inch piece fresh ginger root, very finely chopped
3 tbsp lime juice
1 tbsp sugar
150 ml/¼ pt Greek sheep's yogurt
1 quantity Passion Fruit Sauce (page 217)

With the narrow side facing you, slice the mangoes vertically down one side about 2.5 cm/1 inch away from the centre – you should just miss the stone. Repeat with the other side. Cut off any worthwhile nuggets of flesh still attached to the stone.

Remove the peel and chop the mango flesh. Put two-thirds of it in a blender with the ginger, lime juice and sugar. Blend to a smooth purée, then mix with the chopped flesh in a bowl. Check the flavour and add more sugar or lime juice if necessary.

Spoon into wine glasses, cover and chill thoroughly.

When ready to serve, add a blob of yogurt to each glass (don't stir it in) and spoon over some passion fruit sauce.

TROPICAL FRUIT SALAD

SERVES 4–6

This is a lovely fresh fruit salad for the winter when tropical fruit is easily available and a reasonable price. Make sure the pineapple is really ripe. It should smell of pineapple and you should be able to pull out one of the leaves with a sharp tug. The fruits should produce enough natural juice, but if you like you could add some light Sugar Syrup (page 210) flavoured with lime zest.

1 pineapple
2 mangoes
juice of 2 fresh limes
10 physalis (Cape gooseberries)
175 g/6 oz fresh lychees
175 g/6 oz small seedless red grapes
light Sugar Syrup (page 210) (optional)
shelled pistachio nuts, chopped, to decorate

Peel the pineapple and remove the core. Cut the flesh into small segments and put in a serving bowl.

Peel the mango over a plate to catch the juices. Using a very sharp knife, thinly slice the mango lengthways, starting from one side, until you reach the central stone. Then slice from the other side of the stone. Cut the slices in half crossways. As neatly as possible, cut the flesh still attached to the stone into cubes.

Add the prepared mango flesh and any juice to the pineapple in the bowl. Sprinkle with the lime juice.

Remove the papery husks from the physalis. Cut the berries in half and add to the bowl.

Peel the lychees over a bowl to catch the juice. Make four vertical cuts through the flesh and ease out the stone. Add the flesh and juice to the serving bowl, together with the grapes.

Pour over the cold syrup if using. Chill for 1–2 hours. Sprinkle with pistachio nuts just before serving.

PEPPERED PAPAYA AND PINEAPPLE WITH STRAWBERRIES

SERVES 2

Tellicherry peppercorns are worth looking for. They have a distinctive fresh bright flavour. Don't be alarmed by the combination of pepper, chillies and fruit – the spices add a subtle warmth which really brings out the juicy sweetness of the fruit. Use a very sharp knife to dice the fruit, so that it keeps a distinctive shape rather than turning into a mush.

50 g/2 oz diced papaya
50 g/2 oz diced pineapple
50 g/2 oz diced strawberries
1–2 fresh green chillies, deseeded and finely diced
½ tsp cracked black peppercorns (preferably tellicherry)
pinch of cayenne
juice of 1 lime
juice of ½ orange

Put the papaya, pineapple and strawberries in individual serving bowls.

Combine the remaining ingredients and pour over the fruit. Cover and leave to stand for 30 minutes to allow the flavours to mingle.

GUAVA ICE-CREAM WITH PAPAYAS

SERVES 6

The idea for this simple but exotic dessert came from a Jamaican friend. The combination of guava-scented ice-cream and smooth, velvety papaya is heavenly. Like quinces, the heady fragrance of guavas can fill a whole room. If they are perfectly ripe you can purée them raw, otherwise cut into chunks and simmer with the sugar and water for 5 minutes. Guavas contain very high levels of vitamin C and a good amount of carotene (vitamin A), both known to help reduce the risk of cancer.

3 ripe papayas
lime juice

GUAVA ICE CREAM
150 g / 5 oz sugar
300 ml / ½ pint water
3 ripe guavas, preferably pink-fleshed
strained juice of 1 lemon
200 g / 7 oz ricotta cheese
6 tbsp thick Greek yogurt

To make the ice-cream, put the sugar and water in a small saucepan and stir over a medium heat until the sugar has dissolved. Bring to the boil, then simmer for 5 minutes until syrupy. Allow to cool.

Quarter and peel the guavas, then cut into chunks. Purée in a blender with the lemon juice and cooled syrup, then push through a sieve to get rid of the seeds.

Beat together the ricotta and yogurt until very smooth. Mix with the guava purée, whisking well. Freeze in an ice-cream maker, following the manufacturer's instructions, or pour into a shallow freezerproof container, cover the surface with clingfilm and freeze for about 2 hours until beginning to harden around the edges.

Tip into a bowl and whisk until smooth to get rid of any ice crystals. Freeze again. Repeat the process twice more if time, then freeze until completely firm. Allow to soften in the fridge about 1 hour before serving.

Slice the papayas in half lengthways, then scoop out the seeds, reserving a few for decoration. Remove a small slice from the base of each half so that it sits firmly, and place on individual serving plates. Fill with the guava ice-cream and sprinkle with papaya seeds.

TAPIOCA WITH COCONUT, GUAVA AND LEMONGRASS

SERVES 4

This very refreshing, creamy but low-fat dessert is a far cry from the loathsome 'frog spawn' of school dinners. Serve well-chilled, and use pink-fleshed guavas if you object to a pale grey dessert. Tinned ones drained of their syrup are fine.

2 lemongrass stalks
50 g/2 oz tapioca
1 × 400 g/14 oz can coconut milk
3 pink-fleshed guavas, about 350 g/12 oz total weight
75 g/3 oz sugar
juice of 2 limes
toasted coconut ribbons, to decorate

Remove the coarse outer leaves and bulbous root from the lemongrass. Quarter the tender inner stalks lengthways and put in a saucepan with the tapioca and coconut milk. Bring to the boil, then simmer over a low heat, stirring, for 15 minutes until thickened. Remove the lemongrass and leave to cool.

Quarter and peel the guavas. Cut into chunks and put in a blender with the sugar and lime juice. Purée until very smooth, then push through a fine sieve to get rid of the seeds.

Stir the purée into the tapioca. Pour into a large serving bowl or individual serving bowls. Cover and chill. Decorate with toasted coconut ribbons just before serving.

GRILLED PINEAPPLE WITH GINGER AND LIME

SERVES 4

This is a very quickly made and delicious dessert which needs a ripe pineapple for success. If you want to be really daring, try it with a sprinkling of coarsely ground tellicherry peppercorns. The flavour cuts the sweetness of the sauce in a most agreeable way.

1 small ripe pineapple
4 tsp sugar
coarsely chopped fresh mint, to decorate

GINGER LIME SAUCE
6 tbsp clear honey
finely grated zest and juice of 2 small limes
juice of 1 orange
2 small pieces stem ginger, very finely chopped

Put the sauce ingredients in a small saucepan. Bring to the boil, then simmer for 5 minutes until reduced by half.

Peel and core the pineapple, then slice into about eight 1 cm/½ inch slices. Cut the slices in half, then arrange in a single layer in a shallow ovenproof dish.

Sprinkle the pineapple rings with the sugar. Place under a preheated hot grill, sugar side up, for 5–7 minutes until browned and bubbling. Pour over the sauce and grill for 1 minute more.

Arrange a few slices of pineapple on individual serving plates, and spoon over some of the sauce. Sprinkle with a little mint, and serve while still hot.

GINGERED FRUIT KEBABS

SERVES 4

Use different types of fruit if you like, but choose firm-fleshed varieties which won't disintegrate when heated. The ginger adds a lovely warm flavour, but you don't need too much. Make sure you slice it paper-thin, and use only 2–3 small slices per skewer. Sprinkle the peeled fruit with lemon juice as you work, to prevent browning. This is delicious served with a scoop of Guava Ice-Cream (page 162), and is perfect for a barbecue.

1 small pineapple
1 papaya
2 nectarines
lemon juice
225 g/8 oz firm strawberries
2 cm/¾ inch piece fresh ginger root
50 g/2 oz butter
muscovado sugar

Peel the pineapple, remove the tough core and cut the flesh into even-sized chunks.

Cut the papaya in half lengthways and scoop out the seeds. Slice lengthways into six segments and remove the peel. Cut each segment into three chunks.

Cut the nectarines in half lengthways and ease out the stones. Cut the flesh into neat segments.

Sprinkle the peeled fruit with lemon juice to prevent discoloration.

Rinse the strawberries briefly, remove the green hulls and pat dry with paper towel.

Cut the ginger into paper-thin slices, then cut each slice in half.

Thread the fruit and ginger on to eight metal skewers. Melt the butter and brush over the fruit. Sprinkle with sugar.

Place under a preheated very hot grill or over hot coals, and grill for 5–8 minutes until golden, turning occasionally and brushing with butter. Serve at once.

TROPICAL STIR-FRY

SERVES 6–8

This is a wonderfully blowzy dessert to cheer up a grey winter Sunday. Shake the pan and turn the fruit with tongs, rather than stirring it – that way the pieces of fruit stand a chance of remaining whole. But if it all disintegrates it will still taste just as good. If you don't have all the fruits, use any combination. You will need about 1.2 kg/2¾ lb prepared fruit.

lime juice
1 small mango
1 small papaya
½ pineapple
2 bananas
1 kiwi fruit
50 g/2 oz butter
25 g/1 oz almonds with skin, roughly chopped
1 tbsp sugar, or to taste
150 ml/¼ pint Passion Fruit Sauce (page 217)

First prepare the fruit, sprinkling each batch with lime juice as you work.

With the narrow side of the mango facing you, slice it vertically down one side about 2.5 cm/1 inch away from the centre, so that you just miss the stone. Repeat with the other side. Remove the peel from the two large chunks, then slice the flesh lengthways into long strips. You will be left with some flesh attached to the stone. Either use in a purée, or eat right away.

Halve the papaya lengthways, peel and scoop out the seeds. Cut the flesh crossways into thickish strips.

Peel and core the pineapple. Cut into 1 cm/½ inch thick rounds, and then into chunky segments.

Cut the bananas into 1 cm/½ inch thick diagonal slices.
Peel the kiwi fruit, then slice lengthways into segments.

Heat the butter in a large non-stick pan until foaming. Add the fruit in 2–3 batches with some of the almonds, frying for 1–2 minutes until heated through. Sprinkle with sugar, then transfer each batch to a heated dish while you cook the next.

Finally, add the sauce to the pan and heat through, scraping up any residue. Pour over the fruit and serve at once.

Desserts from a
Mixed Basket

This chapter features desserts made with what I call oddballs – those fruits which defy broad classifications. Rhubarb is not a fruit but a stalk, pomegranates and figs are full of seeds and are neither vine nor stone fruit, Sharon fruit seem more akin to tomatoes, and physalis are from the same family as the tomatillo. However, they all make delicious tarts, fools and compotes, and there are some new ideas too.

RHUBARB

I don't know why, but there is something faintly ludicrous about rhubarb. If it wasn't such a homely fruit, we would surely think it was from outer space with its thrusting pink stems and wrinkly leaves. However, I have recently come around to it in a big way, particularly the early forced variety which I value for being the only fresh homegrown fruit around in early spring. It is grown in Yorkshire in mysterious candle-lit forcing sheds.

Rhubarb is never eaten raw and the leaves are poisonous. The cooked flesh is clean and refreshing. If you can catch it before it falls apart, it makes beautiful compotes and tarts – wonderful served with a scoop of very hard home-made ice-cream.

Choose the young pink forced rhubarb, if possible, as it is less acidic than the thicker maincrop variety. Reject any stalks that are limp or split. Rhubarb will keep loosely wrapped in the fridge for a day or two but soon becomes limp.

Rhubarb contains twice as much calcium as most fruits, although this is much reduced after cooking. Rhubarb is high in potassium and a useful source of fibre too. It contains small amounts of most other nutrients.

Source	Season
Holland	January–September
United Kingdom	January–March (forced)
	April–September (outdoor)

FIGS

Many of us have a problem with figs, having grown up experiencing only the dried form or the dreaded syrup. Fortunately the increasing presence of beautiful fresh figs in supermarkets may help us overcome this prejudice.

Plumply soft, smooth and fleshy, figs were prized by the Greeks and Romans for their aphrodisiac properties. For centuries, they have been an important part of the diet in Mediterranean countries.

The green or purple velvety skins contain thousands of tightly packed edible seeds, opening out to form a crimson flower when the skin is split.

Figs are equally delicious eaten raw, grilled or lightly simmered in a syrup fragrant with spices. You can eat the skin, although some people prefer to discard it.

Figs are incredibly perishable so handle them with care. They are ready for eating when a sticky bead of moisture appears at the base. It's probably better to buy them while they are still slightly firm and allow them to ripen in a warm room. That way there is less risk of damage on the way home from the shop.

Dried figs make an energy-giving snack, or can be soaked, chopped and used in the same way as other dried fruit.

Figs contain useful amounts of fibre, potassium, calcium, iron, zinc, carotene (vitamin A) and B vitamins.

Source	Season
Brazil	May–July
France	July–September
Italy	July–September
Peru	October–January
Turkey	July–October
United States	September–November

POMEGRANATES

The pomegranate is an ancient fruit originally cultivated in the Middle East and Central Asia. It crops up in mythological and biblical stories, and for many cultures was a symbol of religious significance. Described by the French writer, André Gide, as a fruit of 'Pentagonal architecture', the pomegranate does indeed have a fascinating structure. A leathery, yellow or crimson skin conceals tightly packed seeds, each one encased in a translucent ruby cell, or aril. Clusters of cells are divided into sections by a brilliant yellow astringent pith.

I always buy a few pomegranates during their brief season and experiment with different ways of using them. The separated cells make a fantastic jewel-like decoration for all kinds of desserts, or you can heap them into a dish and flavour them with sugar and rose water or wine.

Choose pomegranates with hard, unbroken skins. They will keep for several weeks. The skins will harden but the inside will remain juicy.

Pomegranates are not major suppliers of any particular nutrient, but they contain reasonable amounts of carbohydrate, potassium, iron, B vitamins and vitamin C.

Source	Season
Iran	September–December
Israel	August–December
Spain	September–January

SHARON FRUIT

The Sharon fruit and persimmon appear to be one and the same fruit. Both resemble a large orange tomato with a big greenish-brown calyx. The crucial differences are that an under-ripe persimmon has an extremely high tannin content which sets the teeth on edge, and the skin remains inedible even when ripe. The Sharon fruit is much more palatable. It can be eaten skin and all even when not fully ripe, and it is completely non-astringent. The Sharon fruit was bred from the persimmon and grows in the Sharon region of Israel.

The best way to eat a Sharon fruit is raw. Simply slice off the calyx and scoop out the sweet, jelly-like flesh and seeds with a teaspoon, or cut the skin and flesh into horizontal slices to show off the star-shaped pattern of the seeds. The flesh also makes a luscious purée for fools, ices and cake fillings.

A ripe Sharon fruit will look almost swollen and may have brown spots on the skin. These are a sign of ripeness rather than decay, and the fruit should be eaten within a day or two, or stored in the fridge. Under-ripe fruit will ripen at room temperature.

I think we should eat Sharon fruit more often as a snack. They are extremely rich in carotene (vitamin A), and contain good amounts of carbohydrate, potassium, folate and vitamin C.

Source	Season
Brazil	January–April
Israel	November–February
Italy	September–December
USA	October–December

PHYSALIS

With its papery brown husk concealing a brilliant orange berry, the physalis looks tremendously bewitching, so much so that I feel it ought to be poisonous. Far from it, though – the golden berry is pleasantly tart, sweet and packed with nutrients. The fruit is also known as Cape gooseberry.

They are traditionally dipped in fondant, with the husks still attached but peeled back, and served as an after-dinner *petit four*. You can also add them in moderation to fruit salads or serve them instead of grapes with cheese. Cooked in a light syrup and puréed, they add an astringent fragrance to creamy mousses and fools.

Ripe physalis have a straw-coloured husk and smooth, firm berries. Those with green-tinged husks will ripen at room temperature within a few days, but then need to be eaten immediately or stored in the fridge.

It's a pity physalis are so expensive, for they contain amazingly high levels of major nutrients: carotene (vitamin A), carbohydrate, fibre, potassium and vitamin C. They are also a reasonable source of magnesium, iron and B vitamins.

Source	Season
Colombia	All year
Kenya	June–September
South Africa	September–January

RHUBARB AND SWEET CICELY COMPOTE

SERVES 2–3

Sweet cicely is the traditional herb for sweetening sour fruits. It adds a subtle aniseedy flavour and the green ferny leaves make a very pretty contrast with the vibrant pink of the rhubarb. It's not sold commercially, so if you can't get hold of any, add a few crushed seeds from Chinese star anise pods. It's important not to overcook the rhubarb – one second too long and it can turn to a stringy soup. If this should happen, you can rescue the dish by adding two thinly sliced bananas along with the sweet cicely. They add a pleasing solidity and the sweet flavour goes well with the tartness of the rhubarb.

450 g / 1 lb rhubarb
light Sugar Syrup (page 210) made with 450 ml / ¾ pint water and
75 g / 3 oz sugar
2 tbsp chopped sweet cicely

Trim the rhubarb and cut into 2.5 cm/1 inch diagonal slices.

When the syrup comes to the boil, drop in the rhubarb pieces. Boil for 30 seconds exactly (the rhubarb should still be firm), then drain into a bowl. Put the rhubarb pieces in a serving bowl and return the syrup to the pan.

Boil the syrup for 5 minutes, then pour over the rhubarb. Stir in the sweet cicely and allow to cool. Serve warm, at room temperature or chilled.

RHUBARB AND ORANGE TART WITH STAR ANISE

SERVES 4

The highly perfumed seeds from Chinese star anise pods make a magical combination with rhubarb. The green, unripe seeds from the herb sweet cicely have a similar flavour and could be used instead. For a beautiful shocking pink colour and superior flavour, use forced rhubarb with small leaves. Rhubarb is a useful source of calcium, potassium and magnesium.

1 quantity All-In-One Shortcrust Pastry (page 192) or
Crisp Pastry (page 194)
seeds from 4–5 star anise pods (about 20 seeds)
350 g/12 oz trimmed rhubarb, cut into 2.5 cm/1 inch diagonal slices
2 tsp cornflour
75 g/3 oz caster sugar
finely grated zest of 1 orange
sugar, for sprinkling
low-fat crème fraîche, to serve

Roll out the pastry on a lightly floured surface to form a circle 3 mm/⅛ inch thick. Use to line a 20 cm/8 inch tart tin with a removable base. Chill for 30 minutes.

Meanwhile, crush the star anise seeds and toss with the rhubarb, cornflour, sugar and orange zest. Leave to stand, stirring occasionally, until the juices begin to flow from the rhubarb.

Prick the pastry base with a fork and line with foil and baking beans. Bake in a preheated oven at 200°C (190°C fan oven)/gas 6 for 20 minutes. Remove the foil and beans, and bake for 5 minutes more. Leave to cool.

Spoon the rhubarb mixture into the pastry case. Bake in a preheated oven at 200°C (190°C fan oven)/ gas 6 for 40 minutes until the edges of the rhubarb begin to blacken slightly. Sprinkle with extra sugar just before serving.

RHUBARB AND ANGELICA FOOL

SERVES 4

The sweetly scented stems and leaves of fresh angelica are the perfect partner for rhubarb. Being a sweet herb, it cuts down on the need for sugar. Although not sold commercially, angelica is easily grown. If you can't get hold of any, increase the amount of rhubarb by 75 g/3 oz and add a little more sugar.

600 g/1¼ lb trimmed young rhubarb, cut into 2.5 cm/1 inch pieces
75 g/3 oz fresh angelica stems, cut into 2.5 cm/1 inch pieces
6 tbsp water
150 g/5 oz sugar, or to taste
150 ml/¼ pint whipping cream, whipped
angelica leaves, to decorate
4 small strawberries, to decorate

Put the rhubarb, angelica and water in a saucepan. Cover and simmer over a medium-low heat for 10 minutes. Stir in the sugar.

Transfer the mixture to a blender and purée until smooth.

Divide the mixture among four individual serving glasses. Allow to cool, then chill in the fridge.

Just before serving, stir in the whipped cream, leaving swirls of pink and white. Decorate with a small angelica leaf and a strawberry sliced into a fan.

RHUBARB AND STRAWBERRY FILO TARTS

SERVES 4

Rhubarb and strawberries are a great combination, inspired by a recipe in Alan Davidson's and Charlotte Knox's excellent book *Fruit*. The soft sweetness of the strawberries contrasts well with the acidity of the rhubarb. The dessert is rich in vitamin C and contains calcium, potassium, magnesium, iron and folate. Filo pastry contains less fat than ordinary pastry. Here it is lightly brushed with oil instead of the usual melted butter, which reduces the cholesterol content.

225 g/8 oz trimmed young rhubarb
225 g/8 oz strawberries
75 g/3 oz sugar
2 tsp cornflour
finely grated zest of 1 orange
8 sheets filo pastry measuring 36 × 18 cm/14 × 7 inches
almond oil, for brushing
whipped cream, Ricotta Cream (page 206) or
Low-fat Thick Cream (page 207), to serve

Slice the rhubarb diagonally into 4 cm/1½ inch lengths. Cut the strawberries in half lengthways.

Combine the sugar and cornflour in a shallow ovenproof bowl. Add the rhubarb, strawberries and orange zest, and toss to coat. Leave to stand, tossing occasionally, while you prepare the pastry cases.

Lightly grease 4 individual pie tins, measuring 10 cm/4 inch in diameter and 3 cm/1¼ inch deep.

Stack the filo sheets and cut them into sixteen 15 cm/6 inch squares. Cover with a clean damp tea towel. Taking four squares at a time, lightly brush each one with oil. Place one square on top of the next, slightly rotating each one so that the corners are offset. Place in a tart tin, pressing well down. The pastry should stick up above the rim like flower petals.

Bake the unfilled pastry cases in a preheated oven at 190°C (180°C fan oven)/gas 5 for 10–15 minutes until golden and crisp. Bake the filling at the same time for 15–20 minutes until the rhubarb is only just tender.

Carefully ease the pastry cases from the tins and place on individual plates. Divide the filling between them and spoon over the thickened juices. Serve at once with cream.

FRESH FIGS WITH BERRIES AND RICOTTA SAFFRON CREAM

SERVES 4

This is only worth making with lusciously ripe plump figs, ideally freshly picked and warm from the sun. They look beautiful served on a bed of green leaves, such as nasturtium or vine leaves. Between them, figs and berries are a useful source of fibre, calcium, iron, folate and vitamin C.

12 fresh figs
handful of berries, such as raspberries, mulberries or blackberries, or a mixture
caster sugar
1 quantity saffron-flavoured Ricotta Cream (page 206)

Remove the stalks from the figs. Using a small sharp knife, make a cut like a cross in the top of each fig, cutting almost down to the base. Hold the base with your thumb and fingertips and press gently so that the fig opens out into four petals.

Arrange the figs on a nice white china serving dish or plate. Scatter over the berries and sprinkle with caster sugar. Spoon a soft mound of cream into the centre of each fig.

FRESH FIG AND RAISIN COMPOTE

SERVES 4

Fresh figs have a fragile skin and are easily damaged when cooked. A brief poaching in a medium-density syrup helps to keep their lovely plump shape intact. Serve warm or cold with thick cream, Ricotta Cream (page 206) or yogurt.

500 g/1 lb 2 oz fresh figs
100 g/4 oz raisins
50 g/2 oz almonds with skin
2–3 thinly pared strips of lemon peel
1 bay leaf
1 quantity medium Sugar Syrup (page 210)
3 tbsp grappa or eau de vie, or to taste

Add the figs, raisins, almonds, bay leaf and lemon peel to the hot syrup. Bring to the boil, then simmer gently for 12–15 minutes. Add the grappa or eau de vie at the end of the cooking time.

BAKED FRESH FIGS WITH HONEY

SERVES 3–4

This is a good with slightly under-ripe figs. Choose a dish into which the figs will just fit, pricking them around the base to allow the basting liquid to penetrate. The juice is divine. Serve warm with thick cream, Ricotta Cream (page 206) or yogurt.

12 fresh figs
25 g / 1 oz butter
4 tbsp clear honey
juice of ½ lemon
3–4 small fresh rosemary sprigs
1 tsp orange-flower water (optional)

Prick the figs in several places with a cocktail stick. Set them upright in a shallow baking dish into which they will fit snugly.

Melt the butter and honey together and mix with the lemon juice. Pour the mixture over the figs. Scatter with rosemary sprigs.

Bake in a preheated oven at 190°C (180°C fan oven)/gas 5 for 15–20 minutes, basting occasionally with the juices.

Sprinkle with orange-flower water, if using, just before serving.

FRESH FIG PIZZA WITH ROSEMARY AND PISTACHIOS

SERVES 8

There is no reason why a pizza can't have a sweet topping. Figs, rosemary and pistachios seem in keeping with the Italian nature of pizzas. For a crisp base, cook the pizza on a perforated pizza pan or, better still, a preheated pizza stone. Serve hot with Ricotta Cream (page 206) or whipped cream.

1 quantity Rich Yeast Dough (page 197)
almond oil, for brushing
10–12 ripe fresh figs
25 g / 1 oz shelled pistachio nuts, chopped
3 tbsp mild-flavoured clear honey, such as acacia or orange blossom
1–2 tsp grappa or eau de vie
fresh rosemary sprigs, to decorate

Roll out the dough to a 30 cm/12 inch circle and place on a perforated pizza pan. Lightly brush all over with almond oil.

Cut the figs vertically into 4 slices about 1 cm/½ inch thick. Arrange on the pizza base in overlapping concentric circles.

Sprinkle with the pistachio nuts and drizzle with the honey and grappa. Scatter over a few small rosemary sprigs.

Bake on the top shelf of a preheated oven at 240°C (230°C fan oven)/gas 9 for 15–20 minutes.

SHARON FRUIT AND GINGER GÂTEAU

SERVES 8

An almost fat-free chocolate cake with a low-fat cream filling makes this a richly flavoured but healthy dinner party dessert. Make it ahead of time, wrap in clingfilm and store in the fridge. Try it with papaya instead of Sharon fruit.

50 g/2 oz self-raising flour
25 g/1 oz unsweetened cocoa powder
25 g/1 oz ground almonds
3 eggs
75 g/3 oz caster sugar
6 ripe Sharon fruit
2.5 cm/1 inch piece fresh ginger root, peeled
½ quantity Ricotta Cream (page 206), thoroughly chilled
sieved icing sugar, for dusting

Grease and line a 33 × 23 cm/13 × 9 inch Swiss roll tin with baking parchment.

Sift together the flour, cocoa powder and ground almonds. In a large bowl, whisk the eggs and sugar for 5 minutes until pale and thick. The mixture should leave a definite trail when the whisk is lifted. Fold in the sifted flour mixture. Spoon into the prepared tin and level the surface with a palette knife.

Bake in a preheated oven at 200°C (190°C fan oven)/gas 6 for 12–15 minutes until firm and springy to touch.

Invert the cake on to a wire rack and carefully peel off the baking parchment. Leave to cool.

Meanwhile, peel the Sharon fruit. Roughly chop three of them and put in a blender. Blend to a slightly chunky purée, then stir into the chilled ricotta cream.

Put the ginger in a garlic press and squeeze the juice into the ricotta cream, mixing well.

Cut the flesh of two of the remaining Sharon fruit into small cubes and set aside.

Cut the cake crossways into three rectangles. Lay them on top of each other and trim the edges with a very sharp knife.

Spread half the cream mixture over one rectangle. Scatter with half the chopped Sharon fruit. Place the second rectangle of cake on top, pressing gently with your palm. Spread with the remaining cream and scatter with the remaining chopped Sharon fruit.

Put the last rectangle of cake on top, press gently and lightly dust with icing sugar.

Cut the remaining Sharon fruit into thin horizontal slices. Cut each slice in half and arrange attractively on top of the gâteau.

PHYSALIS PARIS–BREST

SERVES 6–8

This is a lowish-fat but none the less delicious version of a dessert created in the nineteenth century in honour of the famous circular bicycle race from Paris to Brest and back again. I made it in honour of a friend who completed the race last year.

1 quantity Choux Pastry (page 196)
200 g / 7 oz physalis
1 tbsp sugar
1½ tsp powdered gelatine
150 ml / ¼ pint whipping cream
150 ml / ¼ pint strained Greek yogurt
150 g / 5 oz ricotta cheese
icing sugar, for dusting

Spoon or pipe the prepared choux pastry on to a lightly greased baking sheet to form a 20 cm/8 inch ring, about 4 cm/1½ inch wide. If using a piping bag, pipe 2–3 circles on top of each other.

Bake in a preheated oven at 200°C (190°C fan oven)/gas 6 for 30 minutes, or until puffed and golden brown. Do not open the oven door for the first 20 minutes.

Using a long sharp knife, carefully cut the ring in half horizontally to release the steam. Place on a rack and return to the oven for a few minutes to dry out, then leave to cool completely.

Set aside 5–6 plump physalis for decoration. Remove the husks from the rest. Place the fruit in a small saucepan with the sugar and 2 tablespoons of water. Cook over a medium-low heat for 3 minutes until the skins start to burst and the juices flow. The physalis should still hold their shape.

Using a slotted spoon, move the physalis to a bowl. Boil the liquid in the pan for about 30 seconds until syrupy, taking care not to let it burn. Pour over the fruit and allow to cool.

Pour 3 tablespoons of boiling water into a small bowl. Sprinkle the gelatine over the surface and leave until dissolved.

Whip the cream until stiff, then add the yogurt and ricotta and beat until smooth. Drain the physalis and beat the syrup into the cream mixture. Leave in the fridge to set for about 30 minutes.

Spoon the cream over the bottom half of the pastry ring. Arrange the cooked physalis on top of the cream and cover with the top half of the pastry. Dust with icing sugar.

Peel back the husks of the reserved physalis (leaving them still attached to the fruit) and arrange on top of the ring, tucking them into the crevices. Serve at once, or at least on the same day, as choux pastry does not age well.

POMEGRANATES WITH PORT

SERVES 4

This very special and somewhat alcoholic dessert was inspired by Katharine Kagel's recipe for Garnets in Blood, from *Café Pasqual's Cookbook*. Have your guests do the work and let each person prepare their own pomegranate, while you provide napkins and finger-bowls. Seemingly decadent, this dish contains reasonable amounts of iron, zinc and magnesium.

4 ripe pomegranates
150 ml / ¼ pint ruby port or full-bodied red wine
Spiced Sugar (page 211), to taste

Break open the pomegranates and put the seeds in individual glass or white china serving bowls, removing any bits of membrane.

Add 2–3 tablespoons of port to each serving, then add spiced sugar to taste, stirring to make sure it is fully dissolved.

POMEGRANATES WITH SPICED SUGAR AND YOGURT CHEESE

SERVES 2

With their jewel-like seeds, pomegranates are an exquisite fruit, but it's hard to think of things to do with them. They are delicious simply eaten on their own with a sprinkling of sugar, or used as a sparkling garnish for fruit salads. Or try them as here with sweet spiced yogurt cheese. As fruits go, pomegranates are a reasonable source of iron and zinc, and they contain some vitamin C.

1 quantity Yogurt Cheese (page 208) or low-fat quark
½ tsp rose water
1½–2 tbsp Spiced Sugar (page 211)
1 pomegranate
shelled pistachio nuts, chopped

Beat the yogurt cheese or quark with the rose water and enough spiced sugar to taste. Divide the mixture between two individual glass serving bowls.

Using a small sharp knife, cut the pomegranate skin lengthways into four segments, taking care not to puncture the juicy seeds inside.

Take the pomegranate in both hands and break it in half, and then into quarters. Bend the skin back to release the seeds, discarding any bits of membrane.

Sprinkle the seeds over the yogurt and top with a few chopped pistachios.

POMEGRANATES WITH SPICED RICE PUDDING

SERVES 4–6

This is my attempt at re-creating the most delicious rice pudding I have ever tasted. It was served at a large buffet lunch where everyone contributed a dish. Unfortunately I was unable to find out who had made it. It is stunning to look at, with the intense red pomegranate seeds floating in pools of golden syrup on a bed of creamy scented rice.

100 g / 4 oz Thai fragrant rice, well washed
350 ml / 12 fl oz water
850 ml / 1½ pint milk
1 clove
seeds from 2 cardamom pods, crushed
1 tsp orangeflower water
40 g / 1½ oz sugar
¼ quantity heavy Sugar Syrup (page 210), made with golden granulated sugar and flavoured with 1½ tbsp lemon juice
seeds from 2 pomegranates

Put the rice and water in a saucepan, bring to the boil, then cover and simmer over a low heat for about 15 minutes until the water is absorbed.

Stir in the milk, clove and cardamom seeds. Partially cover and cook gently for 1¼–1½ hours until thick and creamy, stirring occasionally, then more frequently towards the end of cooking time, to prevent sticking.

Stir in the orangeflower water and sugar, then pour the mixture into a serving dish. Drizzle with the sugar syrup, then scatter the pomegranate seeds over the surface. Serve warm or cold.

Pastries, Creams, Syrups and Sauces

This chapter gives you ideas for delicious but healthy accompaniments to fruit. There are recipes for pastries and doughs which are either low in fat, or contain polyunsaturated fat instead of the saturated kind that clogs your arteries. There are doughs which trap air, providing lightness and volume, and thus reducing the amount of fat and sugar per serving.

You'll find recipes for low-fat creams and custard-like pouring sauces made with fewer eggs than usual. My advice is, if you occasionally eat cream and custard – say no more than once a week – use proper whipping or double cream, and sauces made with the usual amount of eggs. But if you're worried about your fat or cholesterol intake, and feel a dessert isn't a dessert without some kind of cream, then try these recipes.

There are also recipes for deliciously fragrant fruit syrups and sauces, some admittedly high in sugar – but a little goes a long way. Most syrups and sauces keep well in the fridge for a few weeks, ready to pour over ice-creams and mousses, or to use as a base for an aromatic fruit compote.

ALL-IN-ONE
SHORTCRUST PASTRY

FOR A 20–23CM/8–9 INCH FLAN TIN

There's no escaping the fat in pastry, but using a polyunsaturated vegetable margarine instead of a saturated fat, such as butter or lard, keeps blood cholesterol levels under control. The all-in-one method couldn't be easier. Chilling allows the pastry to relax, so it's less likely to shrink when cooked.

175 g/6 oz unbleached plain flour, sifted
pinch of salt
100 g/4 oz polyunsaturated margarine
1–2 tbsp cold water

Put one-third of the flour into a bowl with the salt, margarine and water. Mix well with a fork. Stir in the remaining flour and knead lightly to form a dough. Wrap in clingfilm and chill for 30 minutes before using.

VARIATION
Ginger Pastry Peel and chop very finely a largeish lump of fresh ginger root. You need 1½ tablespoons of chopped flesh. Put it in a mortar bowl and grind to a paste. Add to the flour with the margarine.

NUT PASTRY

FOR A 23CM/9 INCH FLAN TIN

For extra flavour, spread the nuts out on a baking sheet and toast in a preheated moderate oven for 5–7 minutes until golden and fragrant. Rub off the skins with a clean dry tea-towel. Although undeniably high in fat, nuts contain so many other vital nutrients that they can be justifiably included in healthy desserts.

150 g/5 oz unbleached plain flour
40 g/1½ oz caster sugar
50 g/2 oz shelled nuts, such as walnuts, hazelnuts, cashews, finely ground
pinch of salt
75 g/3 oz polyunsaturated margarine
1½–2 tbsp cold water

Sift the flour into a bowl. Mix in the sugar, nuts and salt.

Rub in the margarine until the mixture resembles fine breadcrumbs.

Add the water and lightly mix to a dough. Wrap in clingfilm and chill for 30 minutes before using.

CRISP PASTRY

FOR A 20CM/8 INCH FLAN TIN

Pastry made with vegetable oil instead of butter or margarine has positive health benefits. It contains very few saturated fatty acids, additives or preservatives. Unlike artificially hardened vegetable margarine, vegetable oils contain no trans fatty acids which are thought to raise blood cholesterol levels in the same way as saturated fatty acids. The pastry is very easy to mix and doesn't need to rest before rolling out. In theory, you could use any vegetable oil, but I find grapeseed or safflower oil give the best results. They are light without any marked flavour, and have the highest polyunsaturated fatty acid content. This is a very crisp pastry. If you want it 'shorter', use a tiny bit more oil.

175 g/6 oz unbleached plain flour
2 tsp caster sugar
pinch of salt
5 tbsp grapeseed or safflower oil
3 tbsp iced water

Sift the flour into a bowl with the sugar and salt. Whisk together the oil and water, and stir into the flour with a fork. Mix to a flaky dough, then knead lightly to make it come together. Roll out very thinly and use at once.

WHOLEMEAL PASTRY

FOR A 20–23CM/8–9 INCH FLAN TIN

With its fibre and mineral content, wholemeal pastry is undoubtedly a healthier option than pastry made with plain flour. However, it can sometimes be depressingly heavy. Wholemeal flour absorbs more water than plain flour, and it is this which makes the pastry tough. Adding baking powder helps overcome the problem, or you can use a half-and-half mixture of plain and wholemeal flour. If you do this, leave out the baking powder. Apple juice concentrate adds flavour. If you don't have any, use an extra tablespoonful of water instead.

200 g/7 oz wholemeal flour or half plain and half wholemeal flour
1½ tsp baking powder (if using all wholemeal flour)
pinch of salt
75 g/3 oz polyunsaturated margarine
2–3 tbsp water
1 tbsp apple juice concentrate

Sift the flour, baking powder and salt into a large bowl, adding the sifted-out bran.

Rub in the margarine until the mixture resembles fine breadcrumbs.

Add the water and apple juice concentrate, and lightly mix to a soft dough. The pastry should not be too damp.

Cover with clingfilm and chill for 30 minutes before using.

CHOUX PASTRY

Meltingly light and airy choux makes the perfect pastry case for all types of fruit fillings. This is one of those occasions when you just have to use butter for flavour. Beating in air adds volume, so there is only a relatively small amount of fat per serving. Use a hand-held electric mixer for the best results. Make the pastry on the day you need it as it does not store well.

100 g/4 oz plain flour
50 g/2 oz unsalted butter
150 ml/¼ pint water, or milk and water mixed
2 eggs (size 2), lightly beaten
1 egg yolk

Sift the flour on to a plate. Put the butter and water in a saucepan over a medium heat. When the butter has melted, bring the mixture to a fast boil. Immediately add the flour all at once, and remove from the heat.

Working fast, beat vigorously with a wooden spoon until the mixture leaves the sides of the pan and becomes smooth and shiny.

Allow to cool for 3–5 minutes, then add the eggs and the extra yolk a little at a time, beating between each addition. Continue beating until the mixture is of a consistency which you can shake off the spoon in one blob. You may need to add the leftover egg white. Use as required.

RICH YEAST DOUGH

TO MAKE A 30CM/12 INCH FLAT BASE

Unlike puff pastry which needs butter to trap air and make it rise, yeasted pastry needs hardly any fat. The yeast acts as a raising agent and traps the air to give a light crisp dough. Oil is used simply to lubricate the dough. Compared with other vegetable oils, sunflower and safflower oil contain extra large amounts of vitamin E and a high proportion of polyunsaturates.

225 g/8 oz unbleached strong plain flour
1 sachet (6 g) easy-blend dried yeast
½ tsp salt
5 tbsp tepid milk
4 tbsp tepid sunflower or safflower oil
1 large egg, beaten

Sift the flour, yeast and salt into a warmed bowl. Make a well in the centre and pour in the milk, oil and egg. Whisk vigorously with a fork, gradually drawing in the flour from around the edge, to form a soft dough.

Knead the dough for at least 15 minutes until it becomes silky smooth and springy.

Put it in a lightly oiled bowl, turning so that the entire surface is coated. Cover with clingfilm and leave to rise in a warm place for 1–2 hours until doubled in size.

FATLESS WHISKED SPONGE BASE

FOR A 26CM/10½ INCH RAISED-BASE FLAN TIN

This is easy to make with a hand-held electric beater. Without this, success depends on spirited whisking – it's the air trapped by eggs and sugar which makes a featherlight sponge. It helps to use eggs which have come to room temperature. Although no fat is used in the mixture, the eggs do contain a fair amount of cholesterol. For a 23 cm/9 inch base, use 50 g/2 oz each of sugar and flour, and 2 eggs.

75 g/3 oz light muscovado or caster sugar, plus 2–3 tsp for sprinkling
40 g/1½ oz plain flour, plus 1–2 tsp for sprinkling
3 eggs
40 g/1½ oz wholemeal flour

Lightly grease a 26 cm/10½ inch raised-base flan tin. Sprinkle with sugar, tilting to coat evenly. Sprinkle with plain flour in the same way, knocking out any excess.

Whisk the eggs and remaining sugar in a deep bowl until very creamy and thick. If whisking by hand, place the bowl over a saucepan of simmering water. The mixture should double in volume and leave a trail which you can still see 5 seconds after the whisk has been removed. Remove from the heat.

Sift the flours over the surface, adding the bran sifted from the wholemeal flour. Lightly fold in with a metal spoon, taking care not to overly disturb the air bubbles you have trapped.

Pour the mixture into the prepared tin and level the surface. Place on a baking sheet and bake in a preheated oven at 180°C (170°C fan oven)/gas 4 for 20–25 minutes until evenly golden and springy to touch. Turn out on to a wire rack and leave to cool.

VARIATIONS

* Add one of these flavourings to the eggs and sugar: ½ tsp vanilla essence, ½ tsp almond essence, finely grated zest of 1 lemon or orange.
* For a chocolate sponge, replace 1 tablespoon of the flour with unsweetened cocoa powder.
* Use all wholemeal flour instead of a half-and-half mixture.

CHEESECAKE BASE

TO MAKE A 23–24CM/9–9½ INCH BASE

Cheesecakes don't necessarily need a base, but if you like the contrast in texture here are a few lowish-fat ideas.

TRADITIONAL BISCUIT BASE
This has less fat than the normal mix. You could use ginger or shortbread biscuits instead of digestives.

225 g/8 oz wholemeal digestive biscuits, finely crushed
75 g/3 oz butter or polyunsaturated margarine, melted

Mix the crumbs and butter until the crumbs are well coated. Press the mixture into the base of a lightly greased 23 cm/9 inch springform tin, pressing it in well around the edge. Chill well before using.

TANGY LOW-FAT BASE
This is a softer base and contains next to no fat. It has a nice tangy flavour.

225 g/8 oz wholemeal digestive biscuits, finely crushed
3 tbsp low-fat yogurt
3 tbsp apple juice concentrate
finely grated zest of 1 lemon

Lightly grease and line the base of a 23 cm/9 inch springform tin.

Thoroughly mix the ingredients. With dampened fingers, spread the mixture over the base, pressing it well into the edge.

Bake in a preheated oven at 180°C (170°C fan oven)/gas 4 for 15 minutes.

CRUNCHY OAT BASE

This is nice and crunchy – a bit like a flapjack.

150 g/5 oz wholemeal flour
25 g/1 oz rolled oats
½ tsp ground coriander
finely grated zest of 1 orange
2 tbsp clear honey
65 g/2½ oz butter

Lightly grease and line the base of a 23 cm/9 inch springform tin.

Thoroughly mix the flour, oats, coriander and orange zest. Melt the honey with the butter and stir into the dry ingredients.

Press the mixture into the base of the tin, pressing it well round the edge.

Bake in a preheated oven at 180°C (170°C fan oven)/gas 4 for 15–20 minutes until golden and crisp.

PANCAKE BATTER

MAKES 450ML/¾PINT, ENOUGH FOR ABOUT EIGHT 18CM/7 INCH PANCAKES

These pancakes are beautifully light, being made with milk and water and only one egg. Leaving the batter to stand allows the starch grains to swell, also contributing to lightness. Adding oil or melted butter not only adds flavour but lubricates the batter so you use hardly any oil for frying.

100 g/4 oz plain flour
pinch of salt
1 egg (size 2)
200 ml/7 fl oz skimmed or semi-skimmed milk
100 ml/3½ fl oz water
1 tbsp safflower or sunflower oil, or melted butter

Sift the flour and salt into a bowl. Make a well in the centre.

Beat the egg with one-third of the milk, then pour into the centre. Mix with a wooden spoon, gradually drawing in the flour from around the edge. Beat until smooth.

Mix the remaining milk with the water, add to the batter and whisk again. Pour into a measuring jug, cover and leave to stand for at least 30 minutes. Whisk in the oil or melted butter just before using.

VARIATIONS
* Add a few drops of vanilla essence or orangeflower water for extra flavour.
* For a sharpish flavour which contrasts well with sweet fruit, use buttermilk instead of milk and water.
* For a lovely nutty flavour use half buckwheat flour and half plain flour.
* For extra fibre, use half wholemeal and half plain flour.

COOKING PANCAKES

Spray or lightly brush a heavy-based non-stick 18 cm/7 inch frying pan with vegetable oil and place over a high heat. When hot but not smoking, pour in about 3 tablespoons of the batter, swirling it around the pan to make a thin even layer. Cook for 1 minute until small holes appear on the surface. Loosen the edges, then carefully turn the pancake over with a fish slice, or toss it if you're feeling confident, and cook the other side.

As you cook the pancakes, stack them on a plate, covering them with foil.

KEEPING PANCAKES WARM

Wrap the stack of pancakes in foil and put in a preheated low oven.

EGGLESS PANCAKES

MAKES 450ML/¾PINT, ENOUGH FOR ABOUT EIGHT
18CM/7 INCH PANCAKES

Perfect for the cholesterol-conscious, these eggless pancakes have a good flavour and a beautiful lacy texture, but they need careful handling. Make sure the oil is really hot. You can buy chick-pea (gram) flour in healthfood shops. It is extremely rich in potassium, iron, zinc and folate. Combined with fruit, the pancakes make a very healthy dessert.

150 g/5 oz chick-pea (gram) flour
pinch of salt
300 ml/½ pint water
¾ tsp vanilla essence
sunflower oil, for frying

Sift the flour and salt into a bowl, then make a well in the centre.

Pour in about half the water. Mix with a wooden spoon until smooth, gradually drawing in the flour from around the edge. Add the remaining water and whisk until smooth. Cover and leave to stand for 30 minutes, then whisk again just before using.

Heat 2 teaspoons of oil in a heavy-based non-stick 18 cm/ 7 inch frying pan until almost smoking.

Pour in a small ladleful of batter with a circular motion, so that the batter is distributed right to the edges of the pan. Quickly smooth the surface with a spatula, spreading it evenly.

Lift the edges when just set and let the uncooked batter run underneath. Fry over a fairly high heat for about 1 minute on each side.

Interleave each cooked pancake with a paper towel, cover with a plate and keep warm while you cook the rest.

SAVARIN DOUGH

TO FILL A 23CM/9 INCH SAVARIN MOULD

Yeast is used as a raising agent to trap air, producing a light and relatively low-calorie dough. Using half wholemeal flour adds fibre without making the dough the least bit heavy. This makes a savarin large enough to serve 10–12, so there is only the smallest amount of butter per serving.

100 g/4 oz strong plain flour
100 g/4 oz strong wholemeal flour
½ tsp salt
1 sachet (6 g) easy-blend dried yeast
150 ml/¼ pint tepid milk
2 eggs
100 g/4 oz butter or sunflower margarine

Sift the flours and salt into a large bowl, adding the bran sifted from the wholemeal flour. Stir in the yeast, mixing well.

Make a well in the centre and pour in the tepid milk and the eggs. Stir with a wooden spoon, gradually drawing in the flour from around the edge. Beat for 5 minutes with an electric beater.

Melt the butter without making it very hot, then beat it into the dough until well absorbed. Use as directed in the recipe.

RICOTTA CREAM

MAKES 300ML/½ PINT

Low-fat versions of cream are usually a compromise. They just don't fall off the spoon with the soft pleasing plop of whipped cream, and the flavour is usually too sharp. But this comes really close to perfection, with about half the fat of single cream and a quarter the fat of double cream.

250 g/9 oz ricotta cheese
3 tbsp low-fat yogurt
½ tbsp sugar, or to taste

Mix all the ingredients in a blender and process until smooth. Use as is or add any of the following flavourings.

FLAVOURINGS
* Saffron: ½ tsp rose water and a pinch of saffron threads soaked in ½ tbsp hot milk
* Passion fruit: pulp from 3 passion fruit and 2 tbsp honey
* Lime: juice and finely grated zest of 1 lime

LOW-FAT THICK CREAM

MAKES 150ML/¼ PINT

This has the thick richness of double cream but contains about one-third of the fat. It's delicious flavoured with grated citrus zest, fruit juice, crushed spices or vanilla essence.

100 g / 4 oz low-fat curd cheese
2 tbsp buttermilk
2 tbsp low-fat Bio yogurt, or other mild-flavoured yogurt
1 tbsp sugar, or to taste

Mix all the ingredients together and beat with a fork until smooth.

BUTTERMILK SAUCE

MAKES 300ML/½ PINT

A light, egg-free pouring sauce with a slightly tangy flavour from the buttermilk. Good with suet puddings.

1 tbsp cornflour
1½ tbsp sugar
150 ml/¼ pint semi-skimmed milk
150 ml/¼ pint buttermilk

Combine the cornflour and sugar, then mix to a paste with a little of the milk.

Put the milk in a small saucepan and whisk in the cornflour mixture. Bring to the boil, stirring, then cook over a medium heat for 1 minute, continuing to stir.

Remove from the heat and whisk in the buttermilk.

YOGURT CHEESE

MAKES 200G/7OZ, 2–3 SERVINGS

This makes a mild cheese, delicious sprinkled with caster sugar
and served with fresh figs or crisp apples.

600 ml / 1 pint low-fat yogurt

Spoon the yogurt into the centre of a large square of dampened
muslin. Gather up the corners and twist to squeeze the yogurt
into a ball. Tie with string and suspend over a basin. Leave in
a cool place to drip for at least 6 hours or overnight.

VARIATION
Ricotta and Yogurt Cheese Mix 200 g/7 oz ricotta cheese with
100 ml/4 fl oz low-fat yogurt. Wrap in muslin as above, and
hang over a bowl for at least 6 hours or overnight.

VANILLA CUSTARD

MAKES ABOUT 450ML/¾ PINT

This contains one egg instead of the usual four or five – a low-cholesterol alternative to traditional custard.

2 tbsp cornflour
25 g / 1 oz sugar
450 ml / ¾ pint semi-skimmed milk
1 vanilla pod, split lengthways
1 egg, beaten

Combine the cornflour and sugar, then mix to a paste with a little of the milk.

Scald the milk with the vanilla pod and leave to infuse for 10 minutes. Remove the vanilla pod.

Add the cornflour mixture to the milk and cook over a low heat for 3–4 minutes until thickened, whisking continuously.

Mix the egg with about one-third of the sauce, then whisk in the remainder. Return to the heat and simmer gently for a minute or two, stirring continuously. Do not allow the mixture to boil.

SUGAR SYRUP

The healthiest and simplest fruit desserts require no extra sugar other than the natural sugars present in the fruit. However, some fruit benefits from a syrup to bring out the flavour, or, in the case of rhubarb and quinces, to make it palatable. I prefer to use unrefined raw cane sugar, either golden granulated or golden caster. This makes a light golden syrup which is a lovely contrast to creamy puddings. If you want a clear syrup use ordinary granulated or caster sugar. The density of the syrup, that is, the proportion of sugar to water, is important. A light syrup with more water than sugar penetrates the fruit more easily and is useful for cooking whole fruits with a dense texture. A more concentrated syrup is useful for soft or over-ripe fruits. Fruit salads rarely need more than the natural juices of the fruit, but some may need a light syrup. A light or medium-strength syrup is used for poaching fruit, while a heavier syrup is used in sorbets and as a glaze for tarts.

LIGHT SYRUP
200 g / 7 oz sugar : 600 ml / 1 pint water, makes 400 ml / 14 fl oz

MEDIUM SYRUP
400 g / 14 oz sugar : 600 ml / 1 pint water, makes 600 ml / 1 pint

HEAVY SYRUP
600 g / 1 ¼ lb sugar : 400 ml / 14 fl oz water, make 600 ml / 1 pint

IDEAS FOR FLAVOURINGS
Citrus peels, juices and oils
Strongly flavoured herbs such as lavender or rosemary
Crushed spices such as cardamom, cinnamon, vanilla, cloves or green peppercorns
Rose water, orangeflower water

To make the syrup, put the sugar and water in a heavy pan with flavourings, if using. Stir over a medium heat until the sugar has dissolved. Brush away any sugar clinging to the sides of the pan with a wet pastry brush.

Bring the syrup to the boil, skim off any foam, then simmer for 5–10 minutes until syrupy. Immediately remove from the heat. Allow to cool a little, then pour into a clean screwtop jar. The syrup will keep in the fridge for several weeks.

SPICED SUGAR

Freshly ground spices permeate the sugar, giving it the most wonderful flavour. Store in a screwtop jar and use to add a touch of magic to yogurt, ricotta cheese or fruit fools, or to sprinkle over the base of pastry cases.

6 cloves
½ tsp tellicherry peppercorns
seeds from 10 green cardamom pods
½ tsp ground cinnamon
350 g / 12 oz sugar

Using a pestle and mortar or a coffee grinder kept specially for the purpose, grind the cloves, peppercorns and cardamom to a powder. Mix with the cinnamon.

Stir the spices into the sugar, mixing well, and store in a screwtop jar.

BLUEBERRY AND LIME SYRUP

MAKES 250ML/9FL OZ

This vitamin C-rich tangy sauce is based on a recipe from Elizabeth Riely's excellent book *A Feast of Fruits*. Stored in a clean screwtop jar, the sauce will keep for 2–3 weeks in the fridge. It's delicious poured over bananas, or chilled and frozen desserts, or stirred into yogurt.

450 g / 1 lb blueberries
100 g / 4 oz sugar
finely grated zest of 1 lime
juice of 3 limes
100 ml / 3½ fl oz water

Put all the ingredients in a saucepan and simmer over a low heat for about 15 minutes.

Push through a fine sieve, pressing the mixture with the back of a wooden spoon.

Line a sieve with two layers of damp muslin and place over a bowl. Allow the syrup to drip through the muslin to remove the seeds (this can take up to 2 hours).

BLACKCURRANT SYRUP

MAKES ABOUT 450ML/¾ PINT

You can make this with bottled or frozen blackcurrants, but fresh ones give a brighter flavour. Blackcurrants are so tart that it's hard to judge how much sugar to use. Taste when the syrup has cooled and add more sugar if necessary. Stored in a clean screwtop jar, the sauce will keep for 2–3 weeks in the fridge.

450 g/1 lb blackcurrants, stalks removed
350 g/12 oz sugar

Purée the blackcurrants in a food processor or blender, then push through a fine nylon sieve, pressing hard with the back of a spoon so that you extract as much juice as possible. You should end up with 300 ml/½ pint.

Put the juice in a saucepan with the sugar. Stir over a medium heat until the sugar has dissolved, then boil hard for about 5 minutes until syrupy.

STRAWBERRY SYRUP

MAKES 300ML/½ PINT

Delicious poured over ice cream, fresh fruit or stirred into yogurt. When you pare the lemon, be careful not to include the bitter white pith. The syrup can be stored in a clean screwtop jar in the fridge for up to two weeks.

450 g / 1 lb ripe strawberries, thinly sliced
150 g / 5 oz sugar
450 ml / ¾ pint water
thinly pared peel of ½ lemon

Put all the ingredients in a saucepan and simmer over a medium heat for 30 minutes.

Strain the mixture through a fine sieve, pressing the strawberries with the back of a wooden spoon to extract the juice.

Return to the pan and boil hard for 5 minutes until syrupy.

VARIATIONS

*   For a subtle burst of warmth, add ½ teaspoon of black peppercorns (preferably tellicherry as they have a brighter flavour) to the pan.
*   Add ¼–½ teaspoon of rose water to the cold strained syrup.

ORANGE AND BAY SYRUP

MAKES 300ML/½ PINT

A friend brought back from Turkey some enormous and beautifully fragrant bay leaves which she found growing wild. I used them to make this scented syrup. Stored in a clean screwtop jar in the fridge, the sauce will keep for up to two weeks.

200 g/7 oz sugar
300 ml/½ pint water
2–3 fresh bay leaves
1 thinly pared strip of orange peel
1 tbsp orange juice

Put the sugar in a saucepan with the water, bay leaves, orange peel and juice. Stir over a medium heat until the sugar has dissolved, then boil for 7–10 minutes until syrupy.

LAVENDER SYRUP

MAKES ABOUT 450ML/¾ PINT

This is an exquisitely flavoured syrup, delicious with ice-cream, sorbets or added to a fruit salad. It will keep for several weeks in the fridge in a screwtop jar.

large handful of lavender flowers
600 ml / 1 pint water
300 g / 11 oz sugar

Shake the lavender free of insects, and put in a saucepan with the water. Bring to the boil, then remove from the heat. Cover and leave in a cool place to steep overnight.

Put the sugar in a heavy-based saucepan. Strain the lavender liquid into it. Dissolve the sugar over a medium heat, stirring constantly. Raise the heat and boil for about 5 minutes until syrupy.

PASSION FRUIT SAUCE

MAKES ABOUT 250ML/9FL OZ

Serve hot or cold with ice-creams, sorbets, pancakes, bananas or steamed fruit puddings. The sauce is particularly delicious poured over hot fruit desserts – the heat really brings out the heady fragrance of the passion fruit. Adding arrowroot makes a slightly thicker sauce, but it is not essential. Although we don't eat them in vast quantities, passion fruit contain a high level of carotene (vitamin A) and useful amounts of magnesium, iron and zinc. Don't discard the seeds – they add a lovely crunch to the sauce, and they are rich in fibre, to an almost laxative effect. The sauce will keep in a clean screwtop jar in the fridge for several days.

8 passion fruit
40 g / 1½ oz sugar
juice of ½ large orange
1 tsp arrowroot dissolved in 100 ml / 3 ½ fl oz water (optional)

Scoop out the passion fruit pulp, including the seeds, and put in a small saucepan with the sugar and orange juice.

Stir over a medium heat until the sugar has dissolved. Bring to the boil, then simmer until reduced slightly.

For a slightly thicker sauce, add the dissolved arrowroot, then simmer, stirring, until the sauce thickens and clears.

RASPBERRY/MIXED BERRY SAUCE

MAKES 200ML/7FL OZ

Quickly made refreshing sauce for pouring over firm fruits, yogurt or ice-cream.

250 g/9 oz frozen raspberries or mixed berries, defrosted
1 tsp lemon juice
1 tbsp icing sugar, or to taste

Put the berries in a food processor and purée until smooth. Push through a nylon sieve to remove the pips.

Stir in the lemon juice and add icing sugar to taste. The sauce should be fairly sharp.

FROSTED FRUITS, FLOWERS AND LEAVES

These are very easy to do and make exquisite decorations for mousses and jellies.

Use grapes, redcurrants, edible flowers such as nasturtiums, rose petals or borage flowers, and herbs such as mint or lemon balm.

Leaving a small stalk attached, paint with beaten egg white, then dip in caster sugar. Place on paper towel on a rack to dry.

Glossary of Ingredients

Most of the ingredients used in the recipes can be found in large supermarkets, good healthfood shops or ethnic stores. A few of the ingredients may be a little unfamiliar but it's worth seeking them out so you can experience new tastes and widen your repertoire.

COCONUT

When using dried coconut, I prefer the flaky ribbons to the desiccated type, which I find too dry. You can buy coconut ribbons in healthfood shops. Toasted briefly in a preheated moderate oven, they make a crispy topping for fruit salads, mousses and fools.

Cans of ready-made coconut milk, or powder which can be made into milk, are becoming widely available. If you buy canned coconut milk, make sure it contains no added sugar.

DAIRY PRODUCTS

Diary products are natural partners to fruit but many of them are high in fat. Fortunately there are acceptable low-fat alternatives – and the emphasis is on alternatives, rather than substitutes. Ricotta cheese, smetana, quark and buttermilk are all naturally low in fat and are delicious in their own way, but a product calling itself 'low-fat double cream' is a joke. The following chart enables you to compare the amount of fat in different dairy foods:

Grams of fat per 100 g/4 oz

Buttermilk	0.5
Cottage cheese	3.9
Cream:	
single	19.1
soured	19.9
whipping	39.3
double	48.0
clotted	63.5
Crème fraîche	40.0
Fromage frais	7.1
Milk:	
whole	3.9
semi-skimmed	1.6
skimmed	0.1
evaporated	9.4
condensed, whole	10.1
condensed, skimmed	0.2
Quark	trace
Ricotta cheese	11.0
Smetana	10.0
Soft cheese:	
full fat	31.0
medium fat	14.5
Yogurt:	
Greek, cow's	9.1
Greek, sheep's	7.5
organic wholemilk	4.45
low-fat	0.8

DRIED FRUIT

Dried fruits are a marvellous standby, especially in the winter months. I like to partner them with fresh fruit too. Try adding small pieces of unsoaked dried apricots to a compote of fresh ones – they add concentrated nuggets of flavour. Or try dried sour cherries in a fresh cherry mousse or ice-cream.

Some dried fruits are treated with sulphur dioxide to preserve the colour and keeping quality, or are sprayed with mineral oil to improve appearance. I use unsulphured dried fruit where possible, otherwise I cover the fruit with boiling water, leave to soak for 1 hour, then drain and soak in fresh water or fruit juice.

EGGS

If I cannot get fresh eggs from a local farm, I use supermarket 'Fourgrain' eggs from chickens fed on a diet of wheat, barley, maize and corn. They have a better flavour and are usually fresh. You can tell a fresh egg by the white – it should be translucent and cling to the yolk. In an old egg the white is clear and watery.

Because of the risk of Salmonella poisoning, desserts containing uncooked egg white should be kept well chilled and eaten within 24 hours. I have not included recipes for desserts containing uncooked egg yolk.

FLOWER WATERS

Rose water and orangeflower water are sold in delicatessens and ethnic stores. They are made from macerated and distilled flower petals and were once commonly used in this country. They are now considered slightly exotic, although they seem to be coming back into fashion. They have always been used in the Middle East to flavour all manner of desserts, cakes and syrups. If you're unfamiliar with these fragrant waters, use less rather than more to begin with, as they can be overpowering.

FRUIT JUICE CONCENTRATES

Available from good healthfood shops, bottled fruit juice concentrates can be used neat to replace sugar and to add extra flavour to fruit salads, ices, mousses and even pastry. Diluted with water, they make a healthy juice drink. They will keep for weeks in the fridge. My favourites are pear juice and exotic fruit juice.

HERBS

Fresh herbs and fruit go well together. The sweeter herbs, such as angelica or sweet cicely, help cut down on the amount of sugar needed for tart fruits. Lemon balm, pineapple sage, rosemary, basil, mint and lemon verbena add zest and fragrance to all kinds of desserts. You will not be able to find all of them in supermarkets, and I hope this will encourage you to grow your own.

LEMONS AND LIMES

In most cases these can be interchanged, but limes do have a very special flavour which I find utterly addictive. I use a lot of zest, meaning the thin aromatic outer layer rather than the peel. For this reason, I buy unwaxed fruit whenever possible, but I cannot understand why these should be more expensive as nothing has been done to them.

The skin of waxed citrus fruit is treated with fungicides to stop it going mouldy. The Government are satisfied that the levels permitted are well within recommended safety limits. However, there is evidence that, in sufficient quantities, these fungicides may produce cancers and mutations in animals. When you use as much lemon zest as I do, you start to worry. If I have to make do with waxed fruit, I scrub it under warm running water and dry well with paper towel, but I'm still not sure how effective this is.

NUTS

Although I have given quantities for the shelled weight, in an ideal world nuts should be cracked just before use as they quickly become rancid. Buy them in small quantities and store in an airtight container in a cool, dry place.

The flavour of nuts is much richer if you toast them first. Place in a single layer in a roasting tin and toast for 3–10 minutes, depending on the type, in a preheated oven at 180°C (170°C fan oven)/gas 4. Stir occasionally until they become golden and smell toasty.

OILS

It is well worth investing in good-quality oils. The unrefined versions are infinitely superior. Sunflower, safflower and grape-seed oils are low in saturated fats and high in polyunsaturates, and are therefore a healthier option. They are light with a neutral flavour, and useful for frying or pastry making. Almond oil is good for greasing baking tins and dishes.

SPICES

Spices add mysterious and beautiful flavours to syrups and fruit compotes. Buy your spices whole and crush or grind them as you need them. They quickly lose their flavour, so buy them in small quantities and store in a cool, dark place.

SUGAR

I use unrefined cane sugar, especially when brown sugar is needed. The manufacturers claim it is a purer product and I'll go along with that.

Index

almonds: black grapes and lychees with almond jelly and lime syrup, 128; fresh fig and raisin compote, 181; gooseberry and almond pudding, 91; khoshaf, 48; red gooseberries with orange and bay syrup, 93; spiced baked apples, 5; tropical stir-fry, 168; yogurt cheese, 62

amaretti biscuits: peach and amaretti ricotta ice-cream, 50; plum and amaretti crunch, 60; yogurt ice with fresh and dried cherries, 55

angelica: rhubarb and angelica fool, 177

anise: gooseberry and almond pudding, 91; grapes with orange and star anise, 134; quince and anise mousse, 26; rhubarb and orange tart with star anise, 176

apples, 1–2; apple, lemon and mint frittata, 10; apple, prune and walnut filo tart, 12; apple and raisin suet crisp, 14; apples in lemon balm jelly, 6; family fruit salad, 17; green fruit salad, 16; spiced baked apples, 5; two-apple pizza, 8

apricots, 35–6; apricot and saffron cheesecake, 40; apricots, prunes and wheat grains in lemon syrup, 46; caramelized apricots with

cardamom and lemon, 44; cranberry and apricot tart, 98; frozen apricot and strawberry savarin, 42; khoshaf, 48; spiced fruit fool, 47

baked fresh figs with honey, 182

bananas, 145–6; baked bananas with clementine and cardamom cream, 150; banana and lemon balouza, 152; bananas with ricotta cream and strawberry sauce, 154; family fruit salad, 17; kiwi fruit and banana slush, 141; strawberry pignolia, 75; tropical stir-fry, 168

basil: melon, strawberry and basil salad, 135

batter pudding, blackberry, 86

bayleaves: orange and bay syrup, 215; red gooseberries with orange and bay syrup, 93

blackberries, 66–7; blackberries with spiced ricotta and yogurt cheese, 84; blackberry batter pudding, 86; blackberry bread and butter pudding, 85; fresh figs with berries, 180; mixed berry kissel, 87

blackcurrants: blackcurrant and cassis granita, 78; blackcurrant syrup, 213; midnight jelly, 79; poached

three-melon sorbet, 138
midnight jelly, 79
mint: apple, lemon and mint frittata,
10; melon cocktail with ginger,
chilli and mint syrup, 132; peaches
with green peppercorns and mint,
49; quince and mint sorbet, 24;
strawberries with orange zest and
Eau de Cologne mint, 74;
three-grapefruit salad with mint,
119
mixed berry: kissel, 87; sauce, 218
mousse: mango and blood orange,
156; nectarine with pineapple
sage, 52; quince and anise, 26
mulberries: fresh figs with berries,
180; salad of dark fruits, 58

nectarines, 36–7; frozen strawberry,
blueberry and nectarine terrine,
76; gingered fruit kebabs, 166;
nectarine mousse with pineapple
sage, 52; salad of dark fruits, 58;
spiced fruit fool, 47
nut pastry, 193
nuts, 223

oats: gooseberry and oat crumble, 90;
greengage and pistachio crumble,
61
oils, 223
oranges, 99–101; blood orange
granita, 120; citrus savarin with
fresh and dried fruits, 112; golden
citrus salad, 104; grape, kiwi fruit
and orange terrine, 130; grapes
with orange and star anise, 134;
grilled pears with orange and
green peppercorn butter, 19;
khoshaf, 48; mango and blood
orange mousse, 156; mango with
citrus salsa, 158; orange and bay
syrup, 215; orange and date salad,
103; plum compote with orange
zest and rosemary, 57; red

gooseberries with orange and bay
syrup, 93; rhubarb and orange tart
with star anise, 176; strawberries
with orange zest and Eau de
Cologne mint, 74; Sussex Pond
pudding, 110; two-apple pizza
with orange and cinnamon, 8
oven temperatures, xvi

pancakes: batter, 202; cherry, 56;
eggless, 204; pear and ginger, 22
papayas, 147–8; gingered fruit kebabs,
166; guava ice-cream with
papayas, 162; peppered papaya and
pineapple with strawberries, 161;
pink grapefruit, papaya and
coconut salad, 120; tropical
stir-fry, 168
passion fruit, 126–7; four melon salad
with passion fruit and chilli salsa,
136; hot passion fruit soufflés, 144;
lime creams with passion fruit,
114; mango and ginger with
passion fruit sauce, 159; passion
fruit pudding, 143; ricotta cream,
206; sauce, 217
pastry: all-in-one shortcrust, 192;
choux, 196; crisp, 194; ginger,
192; nut, 193; wholemeal, 195
peaches, 36–7; peach and amaretti
ricotta ice-cream, 50; peaches in
strawberry rose syrup, 54; peaches
with green peppercorns and mint,
49; spiced fruit fool, 47
pears, 2–3; citrus savarin with fresh
and dried fruits, 112; grilled pears
with orange and green peppercorn
butter, 19; pear and cranberry
compote with walnuts, 23; pear
and ginger pancakes, 22; pear fans
with strawberry dressing, 20;
poached pears in lavender syrup,
18; sautéed pears, 21
peppercorns: grilled pears with
orange and green peppercorn

summer fruit brioche puddings, 82
sunset jelly, 106
sweet cicely: rhubarb and orange tart
with star anise, 176; rhubarb and
sweet cicely compote, 175
syllabub, gooseberry and elderflower,
92
syrup: almond jelly and lime, 128;
blackcurrant, 213; blueberry and
lime, 212; lavender, 216; orange
and bay, 215; strawberry, 214;
sugar, 210

tangerines, 100
tapioca with coconut, guava and
lemongrass, 164
tarragon: strawberry and tarragon
custards, 72
tarts: apple, prune and walnut, 12;
cranberry and apricot, 98; quince
and ginger, 30; rhubarb and
strawberry, 178; spiced medlar tart
with walnut pastry, 32; spiced
quince and cranberry, 28
terrine: frozen strawberry, blueberry
and nectarine, 76; grape, kiwi fruit
and orange, 130
tofu: lime and pistachio cheesecake,
116; lime creams with passion
fruit, 114; quince and anise
mousse, 26
tropical: fruit salad, 160; stir-fry, 168

vanilla custard, 209
vitamins, xi–xii

walnuts: apple, prune and walnut
filo tart, 12; nut pastry, 193;
pear and cranberry compote
with walnuts, 23; prune and
walnut chocolate pudding, 64;
spiced medlar tart with walnut
pastry, 32
weights and measurements, xv–xvi
wheat grains: apricots, prunes and
wheat grains in lemon syrup, 46
wholemeal pastry, 195

yeast dough, rich, 197
yogurt: apricot and saffron
cheesecake, 40; baked cranberry
cheesecake, 96; blackberries with
spiced ricotta and yogurt cheese,
84; cheese, 208; cheese with hot
prune and raisin sauce, 62; guava
ice-cream with papayas, 162;
kiwi fruit and banana slush, 141;
kiwi fruit and strawberry roulade,
140; lime, pistachio and ricotta ice,
118; mango and ginger with
passion fruit sauce, 159; nectarine
mousse, 53; physalis Paris-Brest,
186; plum and amaretti crunch,
60; pomegranates with spiced
sugar and yogurt cheese, 189;
quince and anise mousse, 26;
redcurrant yogurt ice, 89; ricotta
and yogurt cheese, 208; ricotta
cream, 206; spiced fruit fool, 47;
yogurt ice with fresh and dried
cherries, 55